This book was originally written, in 2004, by ex-Superintendent Christopher Bean (Ret) of his experiences in the Colonial Police Forces in Africa during the 50's and 60's. As he was unable to get it published – it being deemed to be too "old" and not very "PC" in today's World – so he only produced a few copies of the manuscript (no photos) for distribution to his family and friends. Christopher later came in contact with "The Federal Saints Group", (the Group started and run by Ian "Witty" Whitfield), of all the ex-Pupils and Staff of the St Andrew's Schools in Blantyre, Nyasaland during the 50's and later. At the request of "Witty" Christopher sent him the text manuscript for inclusion in the "Federal Saints Journal", a monthly publication produced by "Witty" for the Members of the "Federal Saints" Group. After further discussions and the forwarding of all the photographs that Chris had to "Witty" he decided to reconstitute the whole thing into this finished 'book-format' containing all of Christopher's photos and other material that Chris had together with additional material and photos held in the Federal Saints Collection and other sources. It is hoped that this "new" layout and production may result in the publishing of this fascinating book covering "life as it was" in Nyasaland in those days!! We were honoured and privilaged to have permission from Christopher to serialize the book in our monthly Journal and to have been able to work on it converting it to the finished layout as it is now!

– Ian "Witty" Whitfield, South Africa 2012

Bwana wa Polisi

The story of a Policeman's life in England,
Nyasaland and Bechuanaland

1952–1967

Christopher Bean

Published in 2014 by:

30° South Publishers (Pty) Ltd.
16 Ivy Road
Pinetown 3610
South Africa
email: info@30degreessouth.co.za
website: www.30degreessouth.co.za

Photographic Credits:
Christopher Bean
The Federal Saints Collection
ORAFs
Wikipedia, the Free Encyclopedia and Google Photos
The Brereton Collection (held by the Society of Malawi)

Front Cover:
Christopher with his Hunting Dog (a Weimaraner), called "Capucini, (Puci)"
Christopher says "It is the perfect Hunting Dog!"
Photo taken in Gaberones in 1965

Designed & typeset by Pinetown Printers (Pty) Ltd.
Cover design by Blair Couper
Printed by Pinetown Printers (Pty) Ltd., Pinetown, KwaZulu-Natal

ISBN: 978-1-920143-92-3

FOREWORD

This is an account of my life and experiences as a Police Officer, first in the United Kingdom and then in the Colonies. I was fortunate to have a wide variety of experiences which to me seem merely to be a part of my life and not worthy of recounting. Many of my friends however and my family, perhaps weary of hearing my stories over and over again, have begged me for years to commit them to paper. I realise that this may be in the hope that I will stop repeating them!

Even though I consider them to be ordinary for the times and places I was in, my friends who were there with me seem to think that I still have something out of the ordinary to tell, experiences they did not have. It may be that I simply have a better memory than they do. Certainly, anybody living in the United Kingdom who has heard some of my tales can hardly believe them. Ican honestly say that apart from perhaps two or three instances, everything you read in these pages happened to me personally.

Most of the names I have used are the real names of the people involved and I have changed only the names of people who I think may be still alive and might be embarrassed by the stories I have told about them.

Finally, I ask the reader to put aside for the moment, any ideas of "Political Correctness" he or she might harbour. The term was not even invented at the time of my experiences and I write of things as they were, over fifty years ago without condoning or criticising them.

Enjoy my stories, believe them or not, as you wish. If called upon to do so I could probably substantiate all of them.

Christopher Bean
Wakefield, England.
2004

TABLE OF CONTENTS

PART THREE – Bechuanaland 1964–1967

PART ONE – THE UNITED KINGDOM 1952–1957
Chapter One

Nyasaland – How did it Happen?

There I was – sitting on a Douglas DC7B, wearing a thick smart suit, heading for darkest Africa. It was 27th September 1957 and I was 21 years old. I had said goodbye to my mother and father and sister in the morning at Doncaster Railway Station, wondering if I would ever see them again. In those days, Central Africa was a long, long way away and it took two days to get there, in propeller driven aeroplanes. In fact I was never to see my father again as he died before I returned on my first leave to England in 1960. Much was to transpire in those three years and I was to have adventures such as I could never have even imagined during that time. How did I come to find myself in this position?

Well, I have to blame my Dad! He was a Police Officer with Doncaster Borough Police and served his 25 years before retiring, with ill health. During the War he was released by the Police Service and joined the Army with the rank of Captain. He worked in the Allied Military Government of Occupied Territories, (A.M.G.O.T.) and had a healthy taste of high living in North Africa, Italy and Germany. He was demobilised with the substantive rank of Major and returned to the Police Service with the comparatively lowly rank of Sergeant. In common with so many of his compatriots at that time, having served in high ranking positions in the Forces overseas, he found it difficult to settle back to civilian life and for some time looked for ways to work overseas again.

In 1947 he was promoted to Inspector and sent to the Senior Officers' course at the Police College at Ryton-on-Dunsmore.

Whilst there he came into contact with a number of young men who came from the Colonial Police Service and had been sent by their respective Forces to attend the same course. He was impressed with the life style they seemed to be enjoying plus the fact that they all had new motorcars, which they were taking back to their own countries. In those days few British Police Officers of junior Rank could afford cars. He returned from Ryton fully convinced that a career in the Colonial Police was the one his son should follow.

His son however had other ideas and very keenly wanted to become a journalist. Police Officers at that time had a very poor opinion of newspapermen, (I don't comment on their viewpoints today!), and he was vehemently opposed to my idea. He arranged an interview for me with a senior reporter of his acquaintance and this chap, being thoroughly briefed by my

Dad, talked me out of the idea. I still believe that I would have been successful but undoubtedly, would not have had anything like the life I ultimately lead.

This then was my Dad's plan. Get my GCEs, leave school and join the West Riding Constabulary as a Cadet. There was no way he was having me serve in the same Force as him! When I was called up I was to join the Military Police for my National Service and on completing that compulsory two years, rejoin the West Riding as a Constable, serve my probationary period out and then apply for the Colonial Police. And that, more or less, is what happened and how I came to be sitting on that plane. Only more or less though!

Chapter Two

The West Riding Constabulary

In August 1952 I was accepted into the West Riding as a Cadet and did the customary two week course at Wakefield HQ. Having been brought up in a Police household and having heard my father talk so often of his work, I found no difficulty in fitting in to the Police way-of-life and it was only at this time I realised I had a very nearly perfect 'Photographic Memory' as it is called. This stood me in immense good stead throughout my entire working career, especially when I began to appreciate how it could help me. More of that later.

I was posted to Doncaster Division DHQ, so I was able to continue living at home. DHQ was in the centre of Doncaster and so I had close contact with the Borough Force and indeed neighbouring Forces. The job of a Cadet in those days, although serving in uniform, was mainly clerical and I spent my first few months manning the switchboard and being responsible for the teleprinter. One benefit I picked up during this time was a skill in typing. I was sent on a teleprinter course to HQ and before we were allowed on the teleprinters, we had to be able to type at 75 wpm on a manual (!) typewriter. In later years I never had a Secretary who could type as fast as I could!

It was actually a very interesting job because one constantly had to pass messages regarding crime, abnormal loads, Admin matters and so on to the sub-Divisions and neighbouring Forces. I had to liaise with Doncaster Borough, Lincolnshire and Nottinghamshire as a matter of daily routine thus gaining a very in-depth idea of Police Work.

I was of course constantly trying to get involved in 'real' Police Work, volunteering, begging or sometimes being detailed!

One of my regular duties was to don the Chief Superintendent's raincoat over my uniform and go round the corner to the nearest bookmakers to place bets for the officers, including the Chief

Cadet Bean - West Riding Constabulary 1952

Superintendent. Betting shops were of course illegal in those days and we used to bank on the hope that if the Borough raided the "Bookies", as they did regularly, either I would know the officers concerned or my father would intervene. My father was as straight as an arrow and it was unlikely he would have interceded on my behalf. In fact the situation never occurred and in any event I believe by that time most Police Forces warned the "Bookies" they were about to raid them in order for them to get their affairs in order!

I never put a bet on for myself, not having enough money anyway, but in later years when I was a Constable on Race Duty we used to get tips from our mounted colleagues whose horses were usually stabled with the racehorses in those days. It wasn't of course the horses passing tips between themselves but the Jockeys and trainers very often knew that a specific horse just had to win a particular race because there wasn't another horse in the race as fast. Those were sure tips!

Another event, very significant for me at that age, was to attend my first Post-Mortem Examination. I pestered and pestered my Seniors to let me attend one and eventually I was allowed to go to one at Conisborough, a few miles outside town. The Pathologist was very understanding and took care that I was not disturbed although he had no need for concern. One benefit of attending was the fact that the body was that of an elderly man who had died of Emphysema resulting from years of smoking. His lungs were dark yellow and could be squeezed through the fingers. The Pathologist said to me "This is what smoking can do for you lad!".

I never, never had an urge to smoke and never have done.

I learned a lot during that eighteen months or so but was anxious to get on with my life. Still without the desire though to go in the Military Police or join the Colonial Police. I was young, idealistic and undoubtedly stupid. I fancied myself as an Officer in the Infantry. This at a time when Britain was still fighting battles in places as far flung as Korea, Malaya, Borneo, Aden, Kenya, Trieste, Vienna, Germany and Northern Ireland. As an Infantry Officer I could very easily have been killed quickly in any of those places.

Nothing daunted off I went to the Army Recruiting Office in Doncaster, without a word to my father, where I told the Recruiting Sergeant, a huge Coldstream Guard, what I wanted to do. I was in my Police Uniform and when he heard my name he asked if I was related to Inspector Bean of the Borough. On being told I was his son, off he went to my father who was of course furious with what he perceived as my stupidity. The Recruiting Sergeant was also duly briefed and he set about dissuading me from joining any Infantry Units. He said that with my background the Royal Corps of Military Police was the obvious place for me to go. He did however suggest that instead of doing National Service I should sign on as a Regular, the benefits being so much better. Four times as much pay, more leave and travel warrants and some choice as to postings. The period of service however was fifty percent longer than National Service, being three years with the Colours and then four years on the "A" Reserve. This made sense and after completing all the formalities, on 17th November 1957 off I set for Inkerman Barracks in Woking, the home of the Royal Corps of Military Police!

Chapter Three

The Royal Corps of Military Police

The initial training course for the Royal Corps of Military Police was five months long, as opposed to the more usual basic of six weeks for National Servicemen. The course was divided into three sections. The first incorporated the Basic Training mentioned above during which a soldier was taught the principles of marching and drill, weapons instruction – during which he learned to fire a .303 rifle – and general military discipline and procedure.

At the end of this period he had the basic skills of any soldier before specialisation. Then followed a period in the Motor Transport wing, (the "MT"). During this time the Recruit had to learn to drive, either a motorcycle - which was the main means of transport for Military Policemen – or a truck. At the end of this period, all Recruits possessed a full civilian Driving Licence. I qualified on a motorcycle and much fun was had during this time. We learned on old Norton 16H side-valve machines, 500cc single cylinder engines requiring great skill when kick-starting. If the balance on the compression was not right, the thing could kick-back and many a learner was catapulted off the machine by the kick-back. As my entire training period

took place during the winter months, I can honestly say that it was many months before I ever rode a motorcycle on a dry, un-iced road. We had a lot of cross-country work on the Stony Castle Ranges near Aldershot. The Instructors, who were all superb drivers, rode Matchless 500cc twin machines with, wait for it, telescopic front forks! Our bikes had the old girder frames!

The third and longest part of the training was Police Work, Military Law and Procedure and the particular duties of the Military Police. I found this very interesting, and with my existing Police knowledge, not at all difficult. Still, it was with surprise and pride that I learned, a week before we passed out that I had come top of the entire intake, with the highest marks ever achieved at that time by a Recruit! My parents were duly informed and made the long journey

Corporal Bean, Royal Corps of Military Police 1955

down from Doncaster in a borrowed motorcar, together with my sisters, to attend the Pass-Out Parade. This was a fairly long drawn- out procedure involving foot drill and motorcycle displays and so on and the final event was the presentation of Awards.

My father by this time was becoming both bored and somewhat sceptical. He turned to my mother at one point and whispered to her, "Do you think Christopher was bullshitting us?" However came the moment and I marched up to the Provost Marshall, the Officer taking the Pass-Out and duly received the Awards for coming top of my Squad and over-all top Recruit We were then all promoted instantly to the dizzy height of 'Lance Corporal'!

Because of my achievement, instead of an Overseas Posting, I was offered the position of Assistant Instructor in the Depot which I took. I well remember the night before we all left Depot because so many of the newly passed out Recruits were lying in their beds crying! They had been posted to Malaya, Korea, Borneo etc and were sure they were going to die.

Some of them probably did!

I took up my post and commenced teaching fresh Squads what I had learned over the previous five months. For some reason one of the best parts for me was foot drill. I loved, and still love, marching. Especially behind a Military Band!

During this period I took part in the Southern Command Swimming Championships in Aldershot. I won a number of events which was not too surprising as swimming was my major sport at that time. Whilst at school I had represented Doncaster in the County Championships and had swum for Yorkshire Schools. Whilst serving as a Police Cadet I had won a number of events in, and for, the West Riding Police. I competed in all four strokes and was especially proficient in breaststroke and backstroke. My freestyle and butterfly were more than adequate.

Following the Southern Command Championships I was summoned to the Officer of the Major who was our Officer Commanding. After congratulating me he asked me if I had ever ridden horses. I told him that I was a very competent horseman having ridden since the age of five or six years old. He then said he wanted to recommend me for the Military Police Team taking part in the Modern Pentathlon. As far as I can remember, in those days this involved swimming 440 yards, freestyle; riding a horse 5000 metres cross country; running 3000 metres cross country; competing with .22 Match Pistols and fencing with Épées, fighting every other competitor.

This sounded great to me and for four months each of the next two years, I trained in Aldershot for this National Event. For a serving soldier it was a very "cushy" number. We wore civilian clothing, had special rations, had a forty-eight hour pass every weekend – and were incredibly fit. I was only eighteen and nineteen at the time of course. We used to enjoy a very hearty breakfast and then go down to the stables where our horses were waiting, already saddled up and ready to go. We would then ride, cross-country, for two hours, many tumbles and lots of laughs, and finish at 10.00am. Back to the stables and hand over the horses to some other poor chaps to groom and clean-up and off for our NAAFI break. After this we would go to the Command Swimming Pool and swim for an hour. Lunch, then off in the back of a truck to Woking twelve miles away for the rest of our day's training. We would shoot for an hour on the range under the tutelage of an Olympic Pistol Shottist, another NAAFI break and then to the gym for an hour with the Épée, also under an Olympic Coach. The first year this was new to us all and was rather dangerous. Electric Épées were only just coming into being we used them in the real competition, but in training the Épées had a little triple point on the end of the blade. These always seemed to find a way under or through the protective clothing we wore and we all had many a cut on our necks or forearms.

The final "torture" for the day came when at 4.30pm, all our gear was put back on the truck and sent back to Aldershot. We had to run the twelve miles back!!! We used to go to great lengths to avoid this run and would secrete money in our tracksuits and catch a bus if we could get away with it. We would hitch-hike also but this was dangerous because if we were caught out, it was RTU, (Return to your Unit)!!

It was great fun and an even greater "skive" but I have to say, we never achieved any places in the competition. I remember one year, we all drew Lifeguards' horses in the draw for the riding. We drew from a pool in which horses originated in many places. The Lifeguards' horses had mouths and sides like iron and the whole team suffered either falls or runaway horses!

The Royal Corps of Military Police maintained only two sections of Mounted Police, based in Aldershot. These were headed by the legendary Sergeant Scattergood. A wonderful but hard horseman. Having seen the ceremonial duties in which they were involved and watched them patrol at various events, Air Displays etc, skill at Arms Competitions at White City and the Searchlight Tattoo, I fancied a transfer into the Mounted section. This was not difficult to obtain, having been involved in the Pentathlon and I was duly ensconced with the horses. Life soon proved to be very different to that which I had envisaged. Each man was responsible for the maintenance of two horses which had to be exercised and groomed daily. This in itself was an onerous task, starting at six in the morning and finishing at about two in the afternoon, including about two hours actually on the horses! Then the real work started. I was not unaccustomed to cleaning tack but cleaning Military Police tack was a very different story. All equipment in the Military

Police was "bulled" up to a high degree and I was used to it by this time and knew the short cuts. I was forced to acquire a habit which has lasted the rest of my life of always being turned out immaculately. Shoes, even in civilian life like mirrors and trouser creases like razors! Horse tack was another story because after having cleaned the leather and metal thoroughly, it then had to be shined to a mirror finish. The leatherwork, saddles bridles, etc had to be cleaned with Kiwi Military Tan polish and the metal work, stirrups, bits, spurs, sabres and lance heads had to be burnished with a hand-held burnisher until they looked like chrome. As soon as a finger touched the metal, almost immediately a rust fingerprint appeared and of course in actual use, they got wet with sweat, dew and rain. Most of the chaps, instead of spending their pay on booze and tobacco, saved up and took their metal equipment, piece by piece as they could afford it, to a Metal Worker in Aldershot and had them chromium plated. This looked extremely smart and saved many hours of work. A wipe over with a damp cloth and a rub up with a yellow duster and you were done!

On top of this were the hours we were obliged to work. At stables by six in the morning, rarely finished tack before five or six in the afternoon and then very, very regularly, Picket Duties. This meant spending the night in the stables with the horses to ensure their safety. And emergencies were not uncommon. A horse would get straddled over the dividing bar between stalls – almost impossible to sort out by oneself – or a horse might get colic, very dangerous, and once or twice the Picket Guard would be hurt by a horse. I remember one chap going into a stall to do something and the horse kicked him in the head. He was knocked unconscious and lay there the whole night until somebody found him in the morning. He was in hospital for several days and never returned to the Mounted Section. And, of course, the horses did not recognise Christmas, New Year or Easter or any other special days so there always was at least grooming, exercise and mucking-out to be done. After about only four months I realised this was not for me. You had to be 'Horse mad' to enjoy it and much as I love horses, there is a limit.

So, by dent of some manoeuvring I arranged a transfer for myself to Catterick because I had learned the 158 Provost Company, based in Catterick, had a detachment in Harrogate, a mere forty miles from my home and was, in addition, a very "cushy" number indeed. After more manoeuvring in Catterick I finally found myself installed at the detachment in Pennypot Lane, near the Army Apprentice School about three miles outside Harrogate on the edge of the Moors.

Then followed a very idyllic period. There were, I think, about twelve of us there in the charge of a Sergeant and we were responsible for maintaining military law and discipline over the whole of Yorkshire and Co. Durham.

We used to spend long days out on patrol on our motorcycles enjoying the glorious Yorkshire scenery. We could go where we wanted so would often find ourselves in the vicinity of our homes, those of us who came from Yorkshire. In the summer months we found much reason to patrol the Seaside Resorts and also carried out duties at the Royal Yorkshire Show, the Northern Command Tattoo and such events. Winter on the edge of the Moors was a wild experience and much fun, especially on the motorbikes if we could get them on the roads. I remember a lot of snow in those days.

Another aspect of our duties there was picking up Absentees and Deserters, "A's and D's" as we called them. If a soldier, anywhere, with a home address in Yorkshire, either ran away or didn't return from leave, his Unit declared him an 'Absentee'. Notification was sent to the nearest Military Police establishment and in due course we would go out to look for them. We would gather together a few from the same area and leave in the mid-evening by Land Rover. We found that the best time to catch these chappies was in the very early hours, just after midnight and after a call at the local Police Station to advise them of our presence in the area, off we would go to the Absentee's home address. One of us round the back and the other at the front door. Knock, knock, knock, and almost invariably the chap at the back would catch him. They nearly always tried to make their escape through the back door or a back window! We would then take them to the nearest Army Guardroom and hand them over for transportation back to their Units, where, in the most straight-forward of cases they would receive a reprimand or docking of pay. Regular offenders might get some time in detention and those whom we were not able to find eventually ended up being classified as Deserters. We had lots of fun on these expeditions and as a reward stayed in bed as long as we wanted to the next day because we had worked through the night!

Harrogate was a lovely place to be stationed, apart from getting home often, and the town itself was, and still is, beautiful. I was fortunate enough also to develop a very nice relationship with a girl, who worked in the Command HQ next to where we lived. She figured quite a lot in the next couple of years of my life, both in the Army and when I rejoined 'The Riding', but more of this later. I say fortunate because for chaps in the Army getting a local Girl-friend was not that easy. Soldiers didn't have a very good name and the girls tended to steer clear of them. My life was even more idyllic!

My three-years regular service was coming near to its end when fate, and Anthony Eden dealt my very happy existence an unexpected blow! The Suez Crisis developed. The immediate effect on the Army was that regular demobilisations were suspended and the 'Z' Reservists were called up. I well remember laughing because I was "Demobbed" and called up again whilst I slept. On Part One Orders there appeared the item something like,

"2359 hrs. – L/Cpl C.M. Bean transferred to the 'A' Reserve", and on Part Two Orders the item, "0001 hrs. - L/Cpl C.M. Bean Recalled to the Colours".

I slept right through it. What a non-event!!

There were many thousands of these chaps, on the Army Reserve, happily enjoying "Civvy" life, in jobs, married etc and suddenly they were 'Recalled to the Colours'. Many, many of them simply ignored the 'Call to Arms' and were then classified as Absentees. We were run ragged on our "A's and D's" patrols and had a lot of nasty incidents. Many of these people believed very strongly for moral or political reasons that we should not be in Suez and simply refused to go. We usually had to have Civil Police attendance with us.

A further duty the crisis involved us in was ferrying large convoys of troops from all over the country to Southampton for onward transportation to the Middle East. We spent many hours on our motorcycles shepherding long convoys up and down the country.

I cannot leave the Harrogate scene without mentioning the most important case we had to deal with, assisting the Civil Police. Being a District HQ there was a large number of officers and a large Officers' Mess in our camp, together with a reasonably large Military Hospital. The officers either lived in married accommodation with their families, or if single, in single quarters.

In charge of the Hospital was a Major Grace Hogg, of the Queen Alexandra's Nursing Corps (Quaranc). Being single she lived in the Officers' Single Quarters and, as did all officers, and she had a batman, a trooper Edwards. She failed to turn-up for work one morning and later in the day a search commenced for her. There was some concern because her batman had also disappeared. In fact a number of us saw him waiting at the bus stop near our quarters on the morning he went missing. We were involved in a "finger search" of the area, which took two days, and during this search, the natural search of her quarters took place. Not too thorough a search I'm afraid because it took a couple of days more before somebody opened one of her cupboards and found her stuffed inside it. She had been strangled with her own stockings and much violation of her body had taken place. This triggered a Nationwide search for Edwards, terminating when he walked into a Police Station in Blackpool and surrendered. He was tried for her murder and subsequently hanged.

We had all known him quite well, it being a small Military establishment and it appeared that he had several times mentioned to the other batman that he had designs on Major Hogg. The story was that he finally made approaches to her and was of course rejected. It was then that he attacked her. Questions were asked in the House as to why female officers had male batmen and I believe that the practice ceased shortly after this case.

During this time, amongst all our other duties I had been able to go back to the West Riding and have my interview, with a view to rejoining, when I was eventually released. This went well and I remember being very pleased when, as I left the Interview Board, the then Chief Constable, Sir Henry Studdy, who was heading the Board, called me back and said, "Glad to have you back with us Bean". I felt very welcome. The Riding was a big Force and that the Chief could be bothered to make a remark like that made me feel good.

Eventually the Crisis ceased to be one and on one Thursday in October 1956 I was told I was going to be Demobbed the next day. I had the dates of the Training Courses for the next few months at No.3 District Police Training Centre, at Pannal Ash near Harrogate, (fortuitously – Girl-friend-wise!), and my father rang the Riding and I was accepted for the course the next week. I thus left the Army on Friday afternoon and reported for duty at Wakefield, the HQ of the Riding, on the Monday morning next.

A rapid transition indeed!

Capter Four

The Riding Again

On joining The Riding, one first reported to HQ in Wakefield, attested, off to the tailors to be measured up for uniforms and be kitted out and then on the bus to Pannal Ash. There we met up with our Instructors and the other Recruits from other Forces in the area. We comprised two Squads. I was lucky not to be allotted a bed in a dormitory but had one of the small, almost cubicle-like, bedrooms off the dormitories. It was a vast improvement already on the Army where I had been only the previous week. When our uniforms arrived we seemed to have an enormous amount of clothing. Two winter and two summer uniforms, great coats, raincoats and capes, also 'Night' and 'Day' gear. The major differences between 'Night' and 'Day' gear were that all the silver work on the 'Day' uniforms, buttons, helmet badge and so on were black on the 'Night' ones. After the "bull" we were used to in the Military Police, looking after this lot was an absolute doddle.

Anyway, having met-up, been told the form the training was to take, and tidied our stuff away, I was off down to Harrogate to see my girl-friend – much to the envy of my colleagues who were often a long way from home and their girl-friends or Wives! And this was to be mainly the form of my life for the next three months.

R.L.S.S. certificate awarded to Chris Bean

Training consisted of a certain amount of foot drill, which of course I enjoyed and found no difficulty with, physical training in the gymnasium, swimming and Life Saving at Starbeck swimming baths near Knaresborough. The swimming naturally was no problem for me as I already held a National Life Saving Society Instructor's Certificate but a surprising number of the Recruits could not swim and had to learn before they could learn the rudiments of Life Saving. A few never did learn!

Then the real meat of the course was to learn Criminal Law, Police Procedure and Discipline and the Laws of Evidence.

To teach us this we were issued, before each lesson, with a printed précis of the matters to be covered. After the lesson, usually during the evening, these précis had to be copied out by-hand into our 'Blue Books'. A manual about half an inch thick and the size of foolscap. I filled nearly two of these during my training and still have them. These 'Blue Books' were an absolute nightmare for most of the Recruits and they often used to sit until midnight, or later, trying to catch up with their notes, some of them finishing the whole course weeks behind in their notes, with the instructors constantly on their backs!

Now before I left the Army I was entitled to choose a "Rehabilitation" course, to fit me out for life in "Civvy" street. I chose shorthand to complement the typing skill I had acquired on my teleprinter course. I had long wanted to learn shorthand after meeting a Detective, called Leslie Lee, who was stationed at Mexborough, one of Doncaster's sub-Divisions. Leslie used

The R.L.S.S. Swimming Costume Badge

to write shorthand at a rate of 200 words per minute. He used to divide an ordinary shorthand notebook page into sixteen squares and put as much into each square as somebody else would put on a whole page. He thus saved time turning over pages and his shorthand forms were minuscule. Anyway, my course enabled me to write longhand very swiftly indeed. In addition to this I did not smoke, nor ever have, didn't drink tea and so when tea-breaks and smoke-breaks came along, and at lunch time, I was there in the classroom scribbling frantically away to get on top of my notes. It was a rare workday which ended without my 'Blue Book' being up-to-date and after the evening meal, there I was off down to Harrogate again to see my girl-friend! Often I would come back at eleven or eleven thirty and there would be a dozen or more chaps still writing in the classroom. We had to do a kind of guard duty, called "Picket Guard", every so often and these were the only nights I wasn't off down to Harrogate.

I mentioned earlier my near photographic memory and I found that once I had written something in my 'Blue Book', I could recall it easily, even to the extent of knowing where on the page I had written the definition or whatever was being discussed. I was very fortunate in this and my previous Police work, now almost five years back, stood me in excellent stead. It was very obvious that all the ex-Cadets, of which there were a number on the course, had huge advantage over the other Recruits fresh from civilian life.

At the end of each month we had a Major Examination and at each of the first two months, I came top of my class and received a ticket excusing me from Guard Duties.

Off to Harrogate again!

At the end of the third month, a couple of days before Pass-Out, we all had interviews with the Commandant. I was very pleased at mine to be told that I was one of the top three Recruits in the entire intake, not just my class. On the appointed day my parents and sister, my girl-friend and her parents attended the Pass-Out Parade and subsequent presentations. I will never forget, when the Commandant announced the Class Winners and the overall Course Winner as, "PC Bean of the West Riding", there was this concerted gasp of delight from the row near the back where my contingent was situated. I was especially proud because the officer taking the Pass-Out was Sir Henry Studdy, my own Chief Constable! I was also pleased for my father as he was still a serving officer and of course the news got back to Doncaster Borough quickly enough.

The day after Pass-Out our postings were listed on the notice board and I was very happy to be posted to Maltby, a small mining town nine miles from my home in Doncaster. Much further away from Harrogate though!

Police Training Centres

No. 1 DISTRICT PASSING-OUT PARADE

The passing-out parade of the 216th course of recruits was held at Bruche on 28th February, when the inspecting officer was Mr. J. Ormerod, the Chief Constable of Wallasey. There were 38 men and 11 women on parade.

After the address Mr. Ormerod presented prizes to the students who had gained the highest marks in the final examination. They were: P.C. A. T. Windridge (Blackpool) with 93.5 per cent, and P.C. W. K. Owen (Liverpool) with 90 per cent.

The classes gained totals of 65 life-saving and 49 first-aid awards.

No. 3 DISTRICT PASSING-OUT PARADE

On 1st March the passing-out parade of Course No. 131 was held at Pannal Ash. The inspecting officer was Mr. A. E. Godden, the Chief Constable of Wakefield; also present was Sir Henry Studdy, the Chief Constable of the West Riding.

Top places in the final examination were gained by P.C. Bean (West Riding) and P.C. Footitt (Lincs). Winners of the Twenty Questions Police Law Quiz were P.C.s Cutler (Barnsley), Duncan (Nottingham), Ledgard (West Riding) and Ruane (Lincs). The runners-up were P.C.s Renwick and Mallender (Derbyshire) and Footitt and Galloway (Lincs).

P.C. Crank (Rotherham) thanked Mr. Godden for being the inspecting officer and for the advice he had given.

In the evening a most enjoyable dance was held in the Assembly Hall.

Passing-Out Parade notification in the local newspaper

Chapter Five

On the Beat in Maltby

After a weekend's leave, I reported for duty to Maltby Police Station where I was to spend the next year. It was a typical small county Police Station falling under Rotherham DHQ. An Inspector in charge, a Sergeant and about twelve Constables, a couple of them female. To cover all the shifts and leave etc, apart from the Inspector and the Sergeant there were rarely more than two Constables on duty – one manning the Charge Office and the other on the beat in town. Halfway through their shift they would swap jobs. Having gone there as the top Recruit from Pannal Ash I had something of a reputation to live up to – or so I thought! It didn't mean a thing to the other West Riding 'Coppers'. They were very disparaging and soon put the new lad in his proper place. As an indication, I soon found it difficult retaining the relationship with the girl in Harrogate and struck up a relationship with one of the women Constables. Our shifts rarely coincided but when they did, we used to manage a few quick words out of the office,

Maltby - South Yorkshire (from Wikipedia)

Maltby is a Town and Civil Parish in the Metropolitan Borough of Rotherham, South Yorkshire, England, situated in a rural area about 7 miles to the East of Rotherham and 12 miles North-East of Sheffield.

Maltby has its Historical roots in Roman times, and there are several local examples of Roman roads running through the Town. Maltby is mentioned in the Domesday Book as "by-malt", and wa s for Centuries a very small village with the benefits of a fairly large stream nearby and very rich land for Farming available. Since the discovery of Coal in the area in the late 19th Century, however, the population of Maltby has risen from around 500 at the turn of the 19th Century to about 17,980 by the 2007 Census.

Maltby used to be the home to the famous Cricketer Fred Trueman OBE, generally acknowledged as one of the greatest Fast Bowlers in History, who was educated at Maltby Hall School. He moved to Maltby from Stainton with his Parents, and worked at Maltby Colliery as did his Father.

usually in the loo which was next to the little kitchen. The other chaps soon cottoned on to this and my ardour cooled somewhat when I heard that one of them regularly referred to us as, "Them shit-house lovers!!". I soon fitted in however and felt that I contributed to the well-being of the Station. Whilst there I managed to acquire two Commendations from the Magistrates and one from the Chief Constable.

Maltby, as I have said, was a small mining town and as such, pretty rough often. I was never a cricketer but one of my cricketing "Claims to Fame" was that I used to lock-up Freddy Trueman's Mom many a Saturday night. Freddy came from Maltby and was thus a major hero there. His Mom liked her pint of ale and often on a Saturday night would imbibe one or two too many down at the Queen's Hotel, about two hundred yards from the Police Station. The phone would ring in the Charge Office and it would be the Landlord of the Queen's. "Mrs Trueman is performing again. Can someone come and get her please?". Off the outside man would go, pick up Mrs Trueman, who was a trifle loud and uncooperative, wheel her down to the Station and tuck her up in a cell. With the door wide open. Nobody would ever dare arrest Freddy Trueman's Mom! In the morning, we would give her a cup of tea and pack her off home.

I really enjoyed the work of a 'Copper' on the beat and one never knew what the tour of duty would hold in store. It was at Maltby that I delivered my first baby, the first of four, the last being my own second son in Bechuanaland. I was on the night shift, showing the ropes to a Recruit even newer than I was when we spotted a little man scuttling along the skyline at about twelve thirty in the morning. We beat it along to the next intersection and stopped him. He had just been to the phone box to ring the midwife as his wife had gone into labour. To make sure his story was true and he was not some escaping villain, we accompanied him back to his home, a little two-up and two-down mining cottage and sure enough, his wife was in the front downstairs room, very far gone. We said we would wait until the midwife came and sat down with a mug of tea each, (yes, even me). Very shortly after this he came rushing out and said the baby was coming, could we help. Well, in our Basic Training we had been shown film of a birth and told what to do in an emergency. I went in to the bedroom and just managed to catch the baby, a little boy, as he emerged. I cleaned his eyes and air passages and he cried easily. I laid him between his mother's thighs to await,

a) The arrival of the placenta and

b) Even more importantly, the arrival of the midwife.

We had been taught that if arrival of a Doctor or midwife was imminent we should not attempt to cut the cord. Almost immediately the midwife bustled in and almost physically threw me out of the room. "What are you doing in here at this time?" I was speechless and told her I had just delivered the baby but she wasn't having it. My colleague and I beat a hasty retreat before such wrath!

A few days later, I was riding my bicycle, in uniform, down High Street in Maltby when a little chap on the pavement said, "Hey, Hey you!" I stopped, dismounted and with all the majesty of the law and my twenty-one years asked him if he was speaking to me. He said he was and wanted to know my name. I told him it was 'PC Bean' and asked him why he wanted to know and he said, "Wife wants to call bairn after you!" He was the Father of the baby we had delivered so I told him he could call it Christopher, not PC Bean!

Maltby also saw my first encounter with a snake. It was actually a scream and nothing like a forerunner of the many encounters I was to have shortly. A small boy had found this snake, I imagine it was a grass snake, about a foot long. He put it in a jam-jar with holes pierced in the lid and brought it along to the Police Station. Where else? Nobody knew what to do with this snake and eventually it was handed to our CID man to handle! What crime the snake might have committed nobody thought of. He didn't know what to do, didn't know anybody in those days to telephone, so put it in the dog kennel for a while whilst he thought about it. There was never a question of taking it to the edge of town and releasing it. Eventually, the 'Death Sentence' was passed and then the problem was how! Finally this poor little snake was placed, in the jam jar still, in the gas oven in the kitchen and the gas was turned on – unlighted. They tried to gas it but instead nearly gassed themselves as the snake appeared to be impervious to the gas. At last, they beat it to death with a stick. Poor little snake! If it had been one of the six or eight foot cobras, or fifteen-foot pythons which were soon to be commonplace for me, goodness knows what their reaction would have been!

I cannot leave the story of my time in Maltby without mentioning Police Sergeant 1180 Burton. He was our Station Sergeant and the absolute epitome of a superb West Riding Policeman. He was a huge man who drove a little tiny Morris 1000, green in colour. He had a big round face and when he laughed his eyes disappeared behind little slits in his cheeks. His hands were like pounds of sausages and I once saw him, in a fight outside the Queen's Hotel on St. Patrick's night, bang two miners' heads together to get some sense out of them, grip them by the collars both in one hand, and get a third by the scruff of the neck and bang his head on the wall. He was very highly respected in Maltby by both the public and his colleagues. It was he who taught me not to rush into things. He showed me that the best way a Policeman can get control of a situation is not by rushing in but by arriving calmly, speaking slowly and assessing the situation.

One last anecdote about Sgt. Burton, illustrating the difference between Policing in those days and today. We received a phone call to the effect that some lads were smashing windows in a house not far away. I wanted to rush off but Sgt Burton said we must take our time. They would still be there when we got there. And so they were. Three young lads about seventeen or eighteen sitting on a low wall outside this house with all the windows broken. Chewing gum, swinging their legs. Burton, who had probably known them by sight, at least for years said, "Now then lads. What's going on?"

One of the lads, still chewing gum replied, "Don't know Sarge, we've just got here". Wham! So fast I almost didn't see it, Burton hit him with his cape, and a cape was very heavy indeed, an excellent weapon in a skirmish, knocked him, a★★★ over tip, off the wall into the garden. "Now then, I'll ask you again. What's going on?"

"Sorry Sarge, this old biddy has been giving us a lot of cheek so we wanted to teach her a lesson". We took the lads home, their fathers gave them a hiding and they paid for the damage. No time wasted in Court, Justice done, all finished. Can you imagine the uproar over such an incident today? Policing was easy then – and the keepers of law and order were respected – not reviled.

Much as I was enjoying myself at Maltby, I found much of the work tedious, especially making out reports and attending Court. Particularly tedious I found duties at Race Meetings, many of which we had to attend to maintain security. One hot day in August 1957 I found myself once more at Pontefract races, in company with my friend and colleague from Maltby Police Station, Brian Boothroyd. Brian was five or six years older than I was and an excellent Police Officer. Reliable, knowledgeable, educated and I would imagine, destined for higher rank in the Force in due course. It should be remembered that this was in the days before "fast –track" careers existed and it usually took at least ten years to attain the rank of Sergeant and maybe twenty to become an Inspector – all things being equal. Anybody reaching these ranks sooner, even if well deserved, was looked on with great suspicion and had difficulty creating support from lower ranks. This is simply the way it was on those days.

So Brian and I were there, in the centre of the racecourse in Pontefract, hot, dusty and bored. We got to talking about promotion prospects and I mentioned the career my father had envisaged for me. He had not heard of the Colonial Police and was much taken by the concept. In those days advertisements used to be inserted in the weekly 'Police Review' in the middle of the first page inside under the headings, "Crown Agents for the Colonies. Inspectors of Police required for ………". I actually still have the original advertisement we applied for.

We decided that no matter where the next positions were advertised, we would have a go. The very next week there appeared an insert for "Inspectors of Police for Nyasaland". We had no idea where Nyasaland was, in fact we thought vaguely it was in South America somewhere! In no time at all we had applied, completed initial application forms and been invited to the offices of the Crown Agents in Millbank in London. Taking three days leave we set off for London down the old A1 on a big Sunbeam motorcycle and side-car belonging to one of our colleagues on the Station. I had not driven a side-car combination before and we had a very hilarious, and precarious, ride down to London. The many roundabouts then on the road were particularly exciting as I could neither keep the side-car wheel on the road nor pursue a circular course round the roundabout. We got there however and early the following morning presented ourselves to the Crown Agents in Millbank.

As we sat in the waiting room pending our interviews, I noticed a number of leaflets lying on the coffee table and picking one up saw that it described 'The Federation of Rhodesia and Nyasaland'. To our amazement we saw that Nyasaland was in fact in Central East Africa. There was a host of information about the Federation which I quickly committed to memory – my aptitude once more helping me enormously. Thus when I went in for my interview, I was quite well briefed on Nyasaland and its current situation, crops, climate and so on. The Interview Board comprised a Crown Agent, Sir George Martin, the then Assistant Commissioner of Police for Nyasaland, Olly Lodge and an unnamed Civil Servant. They appeared to have little interest in my Police experience and were far more interested in my background and sporting achievements. Swimming for Yorkshire, playing rugby for my town team, (Second Team though it was!), and partaking in the Modern Pentathlon seemed to be what they were looking for. The interview ended after about forty five minutes with the words "We will be in contact Mr Bean".

I left reasonably hopeful and in went Brian Boothroyd. He came out in a shorter time than me and was not so sanguine. When I questioned him it seemed that when asked about his sports and he answered, "I like a game of darts wi' lads", they were not very impressed. When questioned further as to his outdoor activities, he said "Well, I like a bit of cycling!" All in a very broad Yorkshire accent!

The next day we returned on the side-car combo to Maltby and awaited the next step – which was not long in coming. We were on duty at a Race Meeting again, this time the St. Leger meeting in Doncaster and I got a letter saying I was short-listed whilst Brian received one saying the positions were filled. I was, and remain convinced, that his Yorkshire accent and activities failed him the job. I thought this very short-sighted as he was a better Policeman than I was, with more experience but after I had been posted for some time at a bush Station - which I will describe in due course - I realised that at that time, and in that milieu, Brian would have been sadly out-of-place. This situation did in fact change during my time in Nyasaland and applicants' Police Experience received much more value.

In an incredibly short time I had returned to London, had a very full medical examination, been inoculated against everything you could think of and put my notice into the Riding.

One difficulty I had during this time was, (for me), the large amount of money the Crown Agents gave me to kit myself out. Something like a hundred and twenty pounds for excess baggage and one hundred and sixty pounds for "outfitting" myself. This was accompanied by an exotic list of recommended purchases such as a camp bed, a mosquito net, (for a Yorkshireman!), pressure lamps, eating utensils and a host of other things I cannot now remember. I didn't even know where to start looking for most of the items but was saved by one of the chaps from the Station who had just finished a Photographic Course in Wakefield.

He told me that there were three Inspectors from Nyasaland on a Fingerprint course and he had mentioned my impending departure for the Colony.

They showed interest and told him that if I wanted more information, they would meet me in Wakefield one lunchtime and fill me in. A very useful meeting indeed in which I met Brian Graves, John Pallister and Brian Burgess who had just finished their first three-year tour of duty. They gave me a lot of useful tips, chief of which being that I could blow the outfitting allowance on anything I liked as I would never be asked to produce the camping equipment or receipts for it. (How wrong they were to be proved although they could not have known). The Excess Baggage allowance however had to be accounted for down to the last penny.

Somehow, before I left, this lot was spent on other delights and months later when the Secretariat got round to asking me to account for it, I had great difficulty. After much delaying action and a lot of help from my fellow officers I managed to account for most of it – in a fashion!

PART TWO – THE NYASALAND POLICE 1957–1964

Chapter Six

The Nyasaland Police – Zomba

In those days, probably because the aeroplanes all had propellers, the first commercial jets – the Comets - not coming into service for another couple of years, it took two days to fly to Nyasaland. As a contrast, it now takes about ten hours and the planes can fly direct from Lilongwe to Heathrow. The usual route then was to stop in Rome, Athens, Khartoum, Nairobi and then terminate in Salisbury in Southern Rhodesia. Overnight in Meikles Hotel in Salisbury and then fly-on at midday the following day by a Central African Airways Viscount, (more propellers!), to Chileka Airport in Blantyre, the commercial capital of Nyasaland.

Zomba - Malawi (from Wikipedia)

Zomba is a City in Southern Malawi, (formally Nyasaland), in the Shire Highlands. It is the Administrative Capital of the Zomba District.

It was the Capital of first British Central Africa and then Nyasaland before the establishment of the Republic of Malawi in 1964. It was also the first Capital of Malawi and remained so until 1974, when Lilongwe became the Capital. The City is best known for its British Colonial Architecture and its location at the base of the dramatic Zomba Plateau.

I have heard it said many times since, and find it to be absolutely true, that one never forgets the first smell of Africa. It is utterly unique. I stepped out of the DC7 at about 5:00am in Khartoum in the Sudan, wearing my posh, heavy Melton Mowbray suit, (bought with part of the outfit allowance!), into a searingly hot, humid climate. It was like walking into a steaming blanket and the smell was like nothing I had ever experienced. 'Smell' sounds vaguely distasteful but it sounds a little too flowery to call it an 'Aroma'. I have read authors describing it as, "The smell of a hundred thousand cooking fires", mixed up with the smell of the vegetation, rain sometimes, and often exotic flora. Whenever I returned to Africa from Europe, it was always the first thing to tell me I was home and I will never forget it until the day I die. And it is the same smell the length and breadth of Africa - obviously with local ingredients.

I went into the toilets to shave and freshen up and saw my first African, wearing a white Khansu, the strange uniform, skirted, that most servants wore in those days and a red fez, I think there in Sudan it is called a 'tarboosh'. He was without doubt the first African, or black person, I had ever spoken to. I was thus totally without prejudice of any kind and all my subsequent and present feelings about black people were formed as a result of my own personal experiences, not, as is so often the case, by distorted cant issued by

Meikles Hotel – Salisbury in the 50s.

people who have never set foot in Africa or have had two week "orientation" trips.

I eventually arrived in Salisbury at about five in the afternoon, tired and stunned by all the new things I was seeing. I was booked into "Meikles' Hotel" which although I didn't know was classed as one of the 'Great Hotels' of Africa, along with the "Mount Nelson" in Cape Town, "Shepheard's" in Cairo and perhaps "The Norfolk" in Nairobi. My first impressions were of a Hotel in which everything was clean and white, even the Hotel servants' uniforms, and vast rooms with huge verandas as I called them then but which were called there "stoeps". After booking-in I went for a walk around what I could see of the city. Without knowing it I wandered in to what was quite a seedy part along the Manica Road and one in which today a white man would never dare walk. One of the first things to strike me was the abundance of Indian shops with Indian names and goods. Also, I could not understand why the Africans I met walking along the road, always averted their eyes and stepped off the pavement into the gutter until I passed.

In Central Africa, darkness comes around 6pm with little variation the year-round so I soon returned to Meikles. Although I did not drink in those days, I went into the bar for a lemonade and I must say I had never seen, and probably have not since - except perhaps at "Raffles" in Singapore, such a long bar. Not surprisingly it was called the "Long Bar" and again, remarkable for me since I was now in Africa, the only black faces were behind the bar or clearing up tables. Remember there was never a policy of 'Apartheid' in Southern Rhodesia, rather what was euphemistically called a "Culture Bar". In theory a person of any colour was entitled to use all facilities provided he met certain financial and cultural standards. It was to be many years before this came to be really the case. Anyway, after a good meal in the restaurant I was off to bed to be awoken by the very early dawn and the sounds of the Hotel and the city coming to life.

Walking out onto my huge veranda, I was delighted to see that the Hotel actually overlooked a large public garden on the other side of the road. I learned later that it was called "Cecil Square". (No prizes for guessing which Cecil!). The thing about this garden, apart from the fact that it was late September and the grounds were completely covered with a glorious purple blossom from what I later learned were Jacaranda trees, of which Salisbury was full, was the fact that the pathways of the gardens were laid out in the form of the Union Flag. How's that for Empiricism? All beautifully maintained by gangs of Africans already working at that time in the morning.

The old Meikles Hotel was the scene of many famous and Historical meetings and I am glad that I stayed there my first night in Africa, and on a number of future occasions. After breakfast I wandered round the city centre enjoying the space and the leisurely pace and looking at the beautiful shops which abounded. I didn't realise then that Salisbury represented the Mecca of shopping for people living hundreds of miles around, especially in neighbouring territories.

Soon enough lunchtime came and I was picked up at the Hotel and taken to Salisbury Airport for onward transmission to Blantyre in Nyasaland. A short forty-five minute flight in one of the beautiful Viscount turbo-prop planes Central African Airways flew and I landed in Chileka – the "International" Airport serving Nyasaland. I should mention here that although Zomba, forty-five miles away, was the Administrative Capital of the country, the twin towns of Blantyre/Limbe were the Commercial Capital. The white population of Blantyre/Limbe at that time was I think about three thousand. The white population of the whole country was about eight thousand.

As I stepped off the aeroplane I was struck by how much hotter it was than Salisbury had been. It was mid-afternoon on a Saturday and there was very little activity. I was met by an imposing looking white man who introduced himself as Toby Teece, an ex-Sergeant-Major from the Kings African Rifles. He had come to meet me and escort me to Force HQ in Zomba. A black driver Sergeant took my cases and put them in a Police Land Rover and off we went. I should mention here that since setting foot in Salisbury, I had not handled my baggage once. There was always an abundance of black people to carry it for you.

The road from Chileka to Zomba was what is called a single width tarmac, that is a strip of tarmac just sufficiently wide for a car to travel along it and when another car came the other way, both had to veer off and put the nearside wheels on the dirt shoulder. This fifty miles or so of tarmac was all there was in the entire Country for many years to come and we had to learn new techniques of driving on dirt, sand and in mud in the rainy season. The road lead through much cultivated land, many banana plantations, many African villages comprising mud huts, and one of the banes of Africa, cattle and goats loose in the road.

All the many men we passed seemed to be riding bicycles, many highly decorated with all manner of wire contraptions and/or carrying enormous loads on the back carrier. In fact, bicycles were so numerous that Nyasaland was often known as "The Land of the Wajinga", "Njinga" being the Chinyanja word for bicycle. I was puzzled to see that as the Land Rover passed them, all the men dismounted, took off their hats and bowed their heads. Similarly the women, who did not ride bicycles but often carried immense loads on their heads, huge cardboard boxes or vast loads of wood, or then again something as minute as a bar of soap or a small bottle, sank down one knee and bowed their heads. I asked Toby what this was about and he told me it was simply a sign of respect and greeting, not servility and never required by the white people. The Nyasa people were a very courteous people and much in demand "down South" as house servants because they worked so hard, relatively, and were so cheerful and well mannered.

In due course we arrived at Zomba, the capital. It was a delightful small town nestling at the foot of Zomba Mountain. The houses were of course all "Colonial Style", large, surrounded by trees and plants of all descriptions. Again, every house had a very large, often "fly-gauzed" in, verandah stretching right round the house. Here they were called "khondes", the Chinyanja word for veranda or stoep. As in Salisbury, the jacarandas were in full bloom, also a magnificent big tree with scarlet flowers, called a flamboyant. I learned later that all the gardens had an abundance of paw-paw trees, mango trees, avocados and litchis. So many in fact that the gardeners spent their time sweeping up the fallen ones and putting them in compost heaps. Very, very hot and humid, awash with the "Africa" smell and very beautiful!

We entered the Police Camp, as it was called, and went straight to the Officers' Club, where a number of HQ Staff were gathered, it now being close to "Sundown" time. The Club was a long, again typically, Colonial building with a huge welcoming bar. Welcoming that is for those who imbibed and it may be remembered that I didn't and did not for a long time to come either! I was introduced to most of those present, Including the Commissioner, Charles Apthorpe, and after a cooling drink I was taken to the Mess in which I was to live for the next three months. It comprised the first floor of a small block of flats in the Police Camp and was shared between four or five single Inspectors, some of whom had not been there much longer than I had. One

Zomba Plateau

was CID, another Special Branch, one Admin and so on. They explained the set-up to me and I learned that each of them took a month to run the place and take care of catering and so on. At the end of the month the incumbent member reconciled his accounts, divided them by the number of members resident and required payment. We ate well, all the cooking being done by a Nyasa male "Cook Boy", the usual in Nyasaland.

We also each had our personal servant and mine was waiting for me as they had employed him on my behalf prior to my arrival. He was a young chap aged about twenty-five years named Zebio and he received two pounds ten shillings a month plus his full keep and accommodation. Ludicrous as it may seem now, that left him with a tidy sum at the end of the month. These jobs were very highly sought after and included all manner of perks, all the "Bwana's", (the "Boss" or a person senior to yourself), cast-off clothing being but one of them. "Houseboys" as they were called, were always the best dressed of the local Africans.

I was of course very tired by now, so after a shower I retired to my bed, also my first experience of sleeping under a mosquito net. An absolute necessity as malaria was rife.

Before I move on I must mention the malaria problem. As I said it was rife and there were many, many mosquitoes at night. Their noise and frustration at not being able to get through the netting almost kept one awake! And if there was a tiny hole in the netting, which happened often, the houseboy was supposed to find it and repair it, if not the "Mossies" found it! To combat the problem the Government issued all Civil Servants and their families with a Prophylactic called "Paludrine". This was supposed to be taken daily and normally appeared on the breakfast table in a little blue canister. There was another monthly one called "Daraprim" which was not as popular because it was more difficult to remember to take. The mosquitoes of that day were relatively unsophisticated(!) and were unable to penetrate the defence put up by "Paludrine". One had to continue taking it even on long-leave in the UK. It was however totally effective and in spite of being bitten certainly thousands of times in the future years by vast hoards of "Mossies", as we called them, whilst fishing or duck shooting in thick swamps, I never had a trace of malaria. I attribute this totally to never ever missing my daily "Paludrine", because if ever there was a candidate for malaria, as a result of my activities, it was me!

Occasionally one of my friends or colleagues would get a dose and be very, very sick. Sometimes they contracted recurrent malaria which would come back each year without being bitten again. Fortunately at that time 'Cerebral Malaria' was something one never heard of but, after being almost eradicated, mosquitoes and malaria, are now rampant in northern South Africa and

Central Africa again and the "Mossies" are now resistant to nearly all kinds of deterrents. Living in South Africa for the past thirty years, I have known a number of people who came back from a holiday or a business trip to Malawi, Zimbabwe or Zambia to name a few, with Cerebral Malaria – and they die!

Back to Zomba and waking up to heat, humidity, a multitude of birds singing, Zebio bringing me a cup of tea in bed, (and I didn't and don't drink tea!), I really felt I was in Africa. Getting out of bed I saw what I had not seen the previous afternoon, that the town was nestled at the bottom of a beautiful Mountain, appropriately named "Zomba Plateau". The mean height of the land in Nyasaland was about four thousand feet above sea level and the mountain was another three thousand feet higher. A single width road lead up the mountain and operated alternate half-hours up and down. Vehicles could not pass each other and the road lead through magnificent tropical forests to the Plateau on which was a delightful little Hotel called the 'Ku Chawe Inn'. Literally "The Peak". The extra three thousand feet got one away from a lot of the heat and the food in the Inn was very good. The mountain was handled by the Forestry Dept. and there were big pine plantations on the top plus a number of little streams very well stocked with rainbow trout – well used by the local fly fishermen.

I can imagine few more pleasant situations than sitting in the cool of the late afternoon on the shaded khonde of Ku Chawe, one's favourite tipple in hand, looking out across the Palombe Plain to Mount Mlanje about fifty miles away. Mlanje is eleven thousand feet high and over the next three years I got to know it very well.

So, after breakfast one of the chaps took me down to HQ and there I met the Staff Officer, Eric Bult, an ex-Met. Police Officer. He attested me, took me over to the Paymaster/Quartermaster, Alex MacDonald who took me into Zomba to the Standard Bank, opened a current account for me, so I could be paid(!) and then to an Indian tailor to be measured up for uniforms. These took exactly one day to appear and I realised the value of Zebio who already

The Zomba Plateau Clock, showing the times to assend

knew how to handle khaki drill, starch it and press it. He also knew all about polishing shoes and Sam Brownes etc – but so did I with my RCMP background and I fear as far as uniform was concerned, I was a hard taskmaster. These people were however miraculous in the way they looked after our uniform. There were no electric Irons in those days and outside Zomba, Blantyre/Limbe and Lilongwe, no electricity even! The laundry was ironed with an iron heated by charcoal glowing inside it. To keep it hot and glowing the operator would swing the Iron around his head to create a breeze. This sounds somewhat hazardous and indeed was. At fortunately infrequent intervals a piece of glowing charcoal would escape and land on a piece of clothing or bedding. In the case of uniform, this necessitated buying a new item and the ironer was not very popular for a while. As I have said, we were always turned out immaculately and if possible, the black Police even more so. They were wonderfully smart!

Back to HQ and Eric Bult introduced me to a little wizened black Nyasa Inspector, Lester Ngombe, the only black Inspector in the Force, who was to be my mentor in things African for the next couple of months. I spent two hours each afternoon with him, learning the first elements of Chinyanja, the main language, and Native law and custom as it was called.

I realised in later times how invaluable this learning was because, as is obvious, black people are very different to us and to understand some of the differences and why they occur helps one to live more in harmony with them. A few examples follow. White people were very often exasperated by how loud Africans are. A couple walking down the street, next to each other, make a frightful racket, almost shouting to each other. Ngombe explained to me that if black people spoke quietly to each other, people who saw them would fear they were plotting something and view them with suspicion. Speaking loudly showed they had nothing to hide!

I could not believe my eyes when I saw black Constables walking the beat in pairs holding hands! I was utterly horrified until Ngombe told me that African men frequently hold hands as a matter of course and there is nothing sinister in it. On the contrary, if you held another man's hand, it would be more difficult for him to attack you with a spear or a knife!!

One final example of this "Culture Difference" is the way black people will stand very close to you in the Bank or Post Office perhaps. They will stand right on top of you and in more uncertain times this can be a cause for fear, certainly in peaceful times, it is still very disconcerting for a white person. This practice stems simply from the fact that the black people are not blessed with the luxury of space, which we are, and as a result, their "Personal Comfort Zones" (a phrase unheard of then), have different, much smaller parameters. Again, nothing sinister, but annoying to a person who doesn't understand the reasons for this.

My first few mornings were devoted to sitting in the library behind Eric Bult's office studying Standing Orders and the Laws of Nyasaland. Since these were based completely on English Law this was not difficult and Eric was able to point out to me the areas which I would have to study.

My first afternoon after work I was taken down to the 'Zomba Gymkhana Club', the hub of local "Social Life" in Zomba and enrolled as a member.

Zomba Gymkhana Club

The fact that I played rugby and water polo was especially interesting to the Club Secretary. The next day I bought my first car on a Government loan and I was ready to start enjoying life as a "Bwana wa Polisi". (Policeman or literally "Boss" of the Police).

A word about my car and a story forty odd years down the line about the same car. It was a green Ford Consul and of course I was as proud as punch of it. My father was just as pleased and I had managed to achieve what he never managed – ownership of a car. His scheme, planned at Ryton, was working! The Reg. Number of the car was 'BT 6747', 'BT' being Blantyre. I bought it from a chap called Jimmy Kean in the Public Works Dept. He and his wife Maggie, were very sharp, low Handicap golfers. I kept the car for about two years and then sold it on. Cars did not last too long on the dirt roads. Jimmy and Maggie Kean also disappeared from my view and I think they left Nyasaland.

Forty years later I was living in Cape Town and was invited to attend a Reunion of ex-Nyasalanders/Malawians. There were about eighty or ninety people there and after such a time-lapse I knew only a few of them. However I met a chap called Jack Kevitt who had been in the Income Tax Dept. in Blantyre and had been a friend. After all that time we had quite a lot to chat about. He was about to retire as Company Secretary for a very large financial group in Cape Town. We moved into another group together and I met a very good looking woman who was introduced to me as Maggie Kean. The name, but not the face, rang a bell with me and after a while I said to her, "I remember you Maggie. I bought my first car from you in 1957. A green Consul and I can even remember the Reg. No. It was BT 6747". She said she didn't remember me but vaguely remembered the car and congratulated me on being able to remember the number. Jack Kevitt intervened and said it was impossible for that to have been the number of my car as it was the number of his first car. Well we had a heated discussion about it when suddenly I remembered some more. "You fool", I said to him, "of course it was your car. I sold it to you!". Now what were the odds of three different people, all of whom had owned the same car, being in the same room together, thousands of miles away, forty years later? And all remembering it!

I think at this point I will explain the set-up in the Nyasaland Police at that time. Police HQ was in Zomba as I have said, and situated there in the Police Camp were all the expected supporting services. CID, Special Branch, Fingerprints and Photography, Accounts, Stores, Transport and the Police Depot which also contained the Police Mobile Force, (PMF) quick reaction Riot Police trained to deal with civil disturbances which were something new in Nyasaland then. The black members of the PMF were not much trained as Police Officers, although they were attested and were more in the nature of a para-Military Force. Many of them came from the King's African Rifles, (KAR), hence one of the reasons for Toby Teece's presence. The PMF numbered about two hundred Constables and NCOs under the command of a Superintendent, at that time Geoff Yorke and about four Inspectors or Chief Inspectors. It was customary to place new ex-Patriot Officers with the PMF whilst they learned the ways and customs of the black Police, after which they were posted out to a Station.

The Nyasaland Police at that time numbered some three and a half thousand members of whom exactly seventy-five were white officers. I was then No. 75 on the Club Membership list!

I was very surprised to find that of these seventy-five, only about fifteen had seen previous Police Service elsewhere. This was obviously why Brian Boothroyd's Police experience was of minimal interest to them. In fact, as I discovered when I got out onto a Station, Police work was only one facet of the Officer-Commanding a Police District. The country was divided into three Provinces, Northern, Central and Southern, both Administratively and from a Police point of view. Each Police Province was under the command of either an Assistant Commissioner or a Chief Superintendent, and each Province was split up into Police Districts under the command of, at that time, always a white Officer. The manpower of each Station varied considerably depending on the size of the District and its population. Some of the Districts were very large, one or two as big as Yorkshire, and a district that size could have had from eighty to one hundred and twenty Policemen in it. Sometimes in big areas there would be sub-Stations under the command of a black sub-Inspector. Depending on the facilities in the District, the Officer-Commanding could also be, as well as the senior Police Officer, the Immigration Officer, Customs Officer, Game Control Officer, Air Traffic Control Officer, Driving Licence Examiner and anything else that could be loaded onto him!

Back in Zomba, I commenced assimilating myself into the community. Life away from the office centred exclusively round "The Club", and this applied in all Districts. I was soon playing rugby and water polo for Zomba and starting to enjoy a merry social life. Eligible young ladies were in short supply however. The daughters of other expatriates went off to school in the UK mostly, although a few went to Rhodesia or South Africa. When they came home they were

Newly arrived Inspt. Bean

guarded very zealously by their parents and kept away from the ravenous young men looking for female company. We had to make do with the girls in the Secretariat, Nurses, Teachers and such. When I say "make do" I do not mean this derogatively but rather in despair because there were so few of them to go round! Naturally they enjoyed all of this. I found that in most Crown Colonies, Police Officers tended to marry either Nurses, Teachers or Secretaries. I went the usual rounds, in fact I heard Toby Teece telling somebody in the Club that the going question was "Have you been Beaned yet?"

I finally found myself in a situation which I have been dying to call the "Missionary Position!"

Chapter Seven

The Missionary Position

Shortly after I arrived in Zomba the Annual Police Ball was upcoming. This was a major social event, entailing amongst other things, another visit to the tailor to be fitted out with Mess Kit, white "monkey jacket", cummerbund, and also a partner had to be found for me! There happened to be, unattached, at the moment, a very pretty radiologist named Isobel Reid, a Scots girl. Do-gooders paired me up with her and as well for the Ball, I took her out a couple of other occasions, up the Mountain and so on. She was however a couple of years older than me and neither of us was what the other was really looking for. In my case frivolity, in her case something which could lead to more permanence. She did however share accommodation with a twenty year old teacher whom I will call Barbara Parnell. They shared a little rondavel on the lower slopes of the mountain. These rondavels were quite common accommodation in Central Africa and had been developed from the native 'Mud Hut' concept. They were circular and brick built and incorporated a bathroom, a lounge and usually one or two bedrooms. The kitchen in all houses was always outside, next to the back door. Attached to this particular rondavel was a little roofed walkway leading to a smaller rondavel in which was another bedroom and bathroom. It was thus separated from the main rondavel and this was where Barbara lived.

She was a pretty, rather shy girl, and I learned that she came from a Missionary family and her father was in fact still in Missionary Service at a place called Ncheu in the Central Province, about a hundred and twenty miles north of Zomba. We struck up a relationship, one thing lead to another and in no time we were, as they say today, "an item". I want to put this as delicately as I can but I must get across the idea that she took to the physical side of the relationship like a duck to water! Whether it was a natural inclination or the result of a strict, restricted upbringing I do not know, but it was a good job I was a young, very fit man!

I used to leave my car parked at the bottom of their driveway, to make a silent getaway, I would leave via her bedroom window, walk down the drive and coast my car to the bottom of the hill before giving it a rolling-start. Back to the Police Camp at four or five in the morning and spend the rest of the morning with my head down on my desk, snoozing, whilst I had a Constable stationed outside the door to give me warning of anybody coming. Such subterfuges would be totally unnecessary in today's liberal age, but in those days, discretion was very much to be upheld.

After about three months I was posted to a place called Mlanje, some one hundred miles south-east of Zomba and I am not yet at this part of my main narrative but need to mention it to continue the 'Missionary Story'. After finishing work on a Friday afternoon in Mlanje, I was off to Zomba to pick up Barbara and then drive back, a round trip of two hundred miles. When I arrived in Zomba, there was a week's absence, (spelled abstinence!), to make up for before the return trip. On a Saturday afternoon I would usually play rugby and often water polo in the evening, in Blantyre, fifty-four miles away. So more driving.

After a hectic Sunday I would drive her back to Zomba, fond farewells and a long drive back to Mlanje. I had to stop many times on the way and sleep at the side of the road and often didn't arrive back home until four or five in the morning. Back to work at seven thirty. As I have said, thank goodness I was young and fit but even so, the physical side of things started to get on top of me and I was becoming very tired. We decided, to cut out all the driving and separation, and get married. I was twenty-one and she was twenty!!! What did we know?

So, a trip was arranged to visit Ncheu to ask her father's permission. I had been a couple of times before to visit Barbara's family and it was like stepping back at least a hundred years in time! They worked for the United Missions of Central Africa, a Scottish organisation responsible for bringing "The Word" to large parts of Central Africa. The family lived in a collection of what were little more than 'Mud Huts', a kind of very primitive rondavel, next to the Church and the Church buildings. They also ran a little school and a basic clinic and were in fact the only source of facilities for the blacks living for miles around. I came soon to realise that this was in fact all they recognised the Mission for but they had to pay a price. This was it! Every Sunday morning there was held a Church Service. Two or three hundred local Africans would attend. The Church consisted of a thatched roof, low walls about two and a half feet high, and rows and rows of benches for the congregation. Otherwise it was open to the elements. The Pastor, in this case Barbara's father, and his family – and visitors sat at a slightly raised platform facing them.

The Service followed a fairly normal course, hymns and Bible readings and a sermon. I have to give these Missionaries credit for being able to speak absolutely perfect fluent Chinyanja. The sermon lasted at the very least an hour, during which Mr. Parnell, delivered his message with passion. I had great difficulty in concealing my feelings because, apart from the boredom I experienced, the antics of the congregation were hilarious. Almost to a man they fell asleep. You could see their eyes drooping, then shut, and they would flop on the person next to them.

They would then jerk to awareness when they had to sing a hymn and then settle down to sleep again. Mr. Parnell seemed either not to mind or not to notice. The reward they got for their religious fervour, was after a Service of some two hours, a very fine meal was served. I was, and am, convinced that this was the only reason they came. They still believed in their own Gods and witchcraft was rife but you could go and get a good meal if you were prepared to listen to this lot for a while. And time meant nothing to them anyway. What else could they be doing except sleep in the shadows of their huts?

We arrived in the middle of the Saturday afternoon and after an early supper, accompanied by much Grace saying, Barbara and her mother retreated to another rondavel, her mother having been briefed as to the reason for the visit.

After some "umming and ahing" on my part I got stuck in and told him that Barbara and I wished to get married. He showed no surprise and deliberated for a while and then said, "Well, I will have to ask the LORD if you are right for my daughter!". I was a bit stunned and asked him how he would ask. He said, "I will ask HIM in my prayers". (The capitals are not irreverence but to indicate how he answered me!). I asked him when he expected to get a reply and he said, "The LORD will let me know in HIS own good time". I said, "How will he let you know?", and he said, "In HIS own good way!". I tried and tried to get him to give me an answer but he was adamant that he was not going to make the decision by himself – let alone discuss it with Barbara's mother!

We rejoined the ladies having achieved nothing and a little later Barbara and I went for a drive in the bush to look for game, and console ourselves in our own way. After the Service the following morning, we set off back for Zomba rather unhappy at the way things had turned out. Today we would simply have moved in with each other anyway but such a thing was unheard of in those days, in those places!

We returned to our celibate weekdays and frantic weekends but the thrill had gone and the effort was taking its toll. After another month I terminated the relationship, much to Barbara's distress.

You can imagine my amazement some three months later to hear that Barbara had married a Plant Pathologist called, Don Nelson, in Zomba. He was also the Zomba fullback at rugby and a very nice chap. I never understood how he got "approval" so quickly!

Three or four months later I was watching a rugby match in Limbe between Limbe and Zomba and Barbara's husband was playing. I was with my very good friend from Mlanje, Allan Dew, also an Inspector and as we watched the match, Allan suddenly said, "I've got it. That's how they were able to get married so quickly. He got the message intended for you!". This had to be the answer and a few years later I was very relieved that he had got "my answer"!

Having left Nyasaland and Bechuanaland behind, some ten or eleven years later I was living in Bulawayo in Southern Rhodesia and I attended an International Dog Show with my Weimaraner bitch. I met a Veterinary Surgeon named Mike Wright who had lived in Lilongwe and married a Secretary, (what else), named Jill Curtis. They now lived in Lusaka in Northern Rhodesia and had come down with their three Great Danes for the dog show. After exchanging pleasantries and catching up Jill, who had been a bridesmaid at Barbara's wedding said to me, "You don't know how lucky you were - not marrying Barbara!". I asked her why she said this and she told me that the previous year she and Mike had visited Barbara and Don who now lived in Shropshire. Barbara, she said, had turned into an absolute "Shrew" and made Don's life hell!

I privately gave thanks for the inadequacies of the "Heavenly Communication System". But perhaps I could have kept her sweet!

Chapter Eight

The Police Mobile Force

Back to the PMF and Zomba where I soon learned that it was the custom every Friday morning for the entire Unit, to undertake a route march of some ten miles or so.

As the new boy it fell to me to lead the march. I must say that I felt something like Robert Mitchum or his like, marching at the head of a column of some two hundred men. It was also very hard for me, fresh out from England, marching along in a temperature of over thirty degrees. They chose where they wanted to march and a popular choice was to go up Zomba Mountain. Add this to the heat and imagine what I was coping with. After three or four Fridays I learned that this was their way of testing the new "Bwana" and one morning I was thrilled to hear them start singing as they marched. It was utterly wonderful and I loved it! Perhaps not so strangely as they were ex-Army, many of their songs were distortions of British Army songs, even things like "Tipperary", with corrupted, mispronounced words and timing. Their favourite, and mine, was a song originating on the gold mines of Johannesburg, where some of them had worked, and many readers will know it now as the song sung by the supporters of the Springbok rugby team. It is called "Tshosholoza" and sung with deep, deep African voices, it could make you walk through fire! My colleagues told me that they never sang for you until you had proved yourself so I felt very proud to have done so. They were good comrades. Much of the time I was in the PMF I spent asleep at my desk in the MT Section, preparing for inspections by Supt. Yorke, playing rugby and water polo, and escorting the fair Barbara to the Club events or up the mountain and to the Lakeshore. A pleasant initiation into life in the Colonies!

The Queen's Representative in Nyasaland was His Excellency the Governor. Most Protectorates had a Governor although some of the smaller ones had only a High Commissioner. In the case of Nyasaland at that time it was Sir Robert Armitage who held the Post. According to the strict social hierarchy operating in Territories such as this, he was not a person whom a lowly young Police Inspector was likely to meet socially, with a few exceptions. Shortly after arrival in the country one was taken to the entrance to the

The Governor Sir Robert Armitage

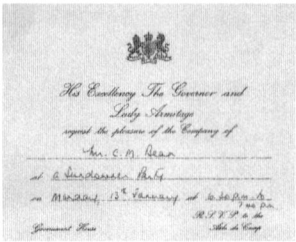

The Governor's invitation

grounds of Government House where there was a rather small guardhouse and one signed the visitors book. Some time afterwards, when "H.E.", (as he was called), held his next official Sundowner Party, a very impressive invitation card embossed with the Royal Coat of Arms would arrive requesting one's presence at the party, the visitors' book being the source of the guest list. I still have my first Invitation. Of course, it was not 'done', then, to refuse such an invitation, and who would want to anyway, and so, in theory, provided they had signed the book, every new arrival, and a sprinkling of local established, residents, both Government and commercial, would be able to meet the Queen's Representative.

As is the way with these things, it is highly unlikely that he would remember the meeting!

I must say I thought it was all very grand at that stage and was most impressed with the people I met and the interior of Government House. Really it was just a well appointed large Colonial House and the people attending were the usual mix of people in awe, people who drank too much and had a careful eye kept on them by discreet officials, and as I later learned, people who were having affairs with other people's wives. Let's face it – there wasn't much else to do to liven up social life there!

In January 1958 an event occurred which gave me a brief closer encounter with "H.E." and Government House. The guard for the house and grounds was traditionally provided by the Kings African Rifles, (K.A.R.) of which there was one Battalion stationed in Lusaka in Northern Rhodesia and one in Nyasaland, in Zomba. Every three years they rotated and when this rotation took place they were too busy to provide the Government House guard at which time the Police Mobile Force, (PMF) took over the responsibility. This involved much serious practising and a number of teams of guards were selected and trained. Apart from having to patrol the grounds of Government House, they also had to provide the 'Honour Guard' at the main entrance. As one of the officers charged with being Officer-in-Charge of the guard, I had to be shown the interior of the House in order to be able to go quickly to the

Government House

seat of any possible incident so I saw a lot more of the House than many of my colleagues. From a point of view of show, the Honour Guard was the most important and we spent many hours practising the "Turn-out" and salute. The way this worked was that when the Governor was about to leave the House, somebody telephoned down to the guardhouse and said he wasleaving shortly. The Sergeant on duty would keep his eyes sharply open and as the Rolls Royce came round the last bend of trees and hove into view, a quick order was given and out would tumble the guard, dress smartly from the right, and as the car passed, they would 'Present Arms'. Afterwards it was 'Slope Arms' and back into the guardhouse until his return. A very, very simple little ceremony but our O.C., Geoff Yorke, insisted it had to be perfect in every respect. So we rehearsed and rehearsed at one of the Police Camp guardhouses and I remember that I usually took the part of the Governor and drove my little Ford Consul past the guard. I would sit about two hundred yards back and when they were ready to turn out, Bwana wa Polisi Yorke would wave his swagger stick and leather gloves, (he always dressed the part!), at me and I would sedately approach and out would turn the guard. The Ford Consul of those days started with a knob under the centre of the fascia which one pulled to start the motor. On one occasion, I pulled the knob on Yorke's signal, and "it came off in me 'and Governor". I was left with a knob and about a yard of thin steel cable and a stationary car! Yorke, who was pretty choleric at the best of times, was virtually frothing at the mouth and waving frantically. Eventually a runner was despatched to ascertain the problem and shortly afterwards, four strong Constables came to give me a push. A not very auspicious start to the event but in fact, it all went swimmingly and I even have this old photo of the guard house with a resplendent guard turned out and a very young, slender, vigilant Inspector Bean on the job!

Nyasaland Police on guard duty at the entrance to Government House, Christopher Bean pictured on the left. (Jan 1958)

Chapter Nine

Lake Nyasa

Lake Malawi
(From Wikipedia)

Lake Malawi, (also known as Lake Nyasa), is an African Great Lake and the Southernmost Lake in the East African Rift system. This Lake, the third largest in Africa and the eighth largest in the World, is located between Malawi, Mozambique, and Tanzania. It is the second deepest Lake in Africa, although its placid Northern shore gives no hint of its depth. This Great Lake's Tropical waters are reportedly the habitat of more species of Fish than those of any other body of freshwater on Earth, including more than 1000 species of Cichlids.

Lake Malawi was officially declared a Reserve by the Government of Mozambique on June 10, 2011 in an effort to protect one of the largest and biodiverse Freshwater Lakes in the World.

I cannot leave Zomba without mention of Lake Nyasa, (or Lake Malawi as it is now called). The nearest part of the Lake was situated about a hundred and twenty miles or three or four hours drive, in good weather, from Zomba. The road was all dirt from Zomba northwards and not far north was the first hazard, the Kasupe Escarpment. In rainy weather this was an absolute nightmare and many a car spent the night or day there until rescue came. About thirty miles further north one came to the Shire River, (pronounced "Shirry" as in "Sherry", not "Shire" as in "Yorkshire"), which is the only exit from the Lake and wended its way down through southern Nyasaland until it merged with the Zambezi in Portuguese East Africa. The Shire is a very large, exciting, typically tropical African river and at the point where the road north crosses it, at Liwonde, it is about seventy or eighty yards wide. The river teemed with crocodiles and hippo and they were a very common sight. At that time, and for many years afterwards, it was crossed by a type of Ferry, very common, perhaps still even now in Africa. This consisted of a very heavy rope stretching from bank-to-bank to which was attached a large pontoon which could carry perhaps six cars, or a couple of heavy lorries or a bus, or a combination of these. Power was provided by several Africans who, whilst being on the Ferry, hauled it across by pulling on the rope which stretched between the banks. They literally "walked" the Ferry across by holding the rope while walking towards the rear of the Ferry and when they reached there they let go of the rope and walked back in rotation to the front, grabbed

the rope again and repeated the exercise. The crossing took only five or six minutes but the wait to get on the Ferry sometimes took as much as five or six hours if one arrived when there was a big queue of trucks and buses!

The Liwonde Ferry

This state of affairs continued for several years after I left Nyasaland until one day following one of the interminable political meetings which took place then, in Zomba, as is common in these places, they overloaded the Ferry with two buses which were themselves overloaded with people going to the meeting. In the middle of the crossing, the Ferry overturned depositing something like two hundred Africans into the river. The crocodiles went mad and people said they had never seen so many crocodiles in one place at the same time. The commotion in turn attracted even more crocs and they came from far and wide to feast. It was estimated that one hundred and forty seven Africans were lost to the crocs that day!

As a result of this funds were quickly made available by the United Nations or some Charitable Aid Fund and a splendid 'Bund' was built across the Shire which acted not only as sluice gates to control the Lake level but also as a convenient "Bridge" across the river making the old Ferry obsolete.

When travelling by road from Nyasaland to Southern Rhodesia, through Portuguese East Africa (P.E.A.), a similar problem occurred when one came to Tete on the Zambezi River. The Zambezi is no "play-play" river – it is a serious river and crossing it is an adventure. There was a Ferry there also but because the river is so much wider there, sometimes a mile wide, a powerful launch pulled the same type of Ferry across. The hazard there was not so much that the Ferry might turn-over but the launch's engine would regularly fail or sometimes, the tow chain parted. The Ferry was then left to its own devices and would often meander miles down river or until it became marooned on a sandbank. Eventually the launch, either with its engine repaired, or with a new chain, or even a relief launch would catch the Ferry up and laboriously tow it back up river until it reached Tete. And it was common to wait two or three days sometimes to get on that Ferry! Journeys in "Wild Africa" were not to be undertaken by the faint-hearted in those days, even with the advent

The Liwonde 'Bund' with the gates open

Palm Beach Hotel on the lake shore

of motor cars! Salisbury was only four hundred miles from Blantyre, all dirt road, and one usually allowed two days for the trip but often it took four or five! A magnificent bridge has now been built there.

Anyway, having crossed the Ferry at Liwonde there was a further sixty or seventy miles until one reached Palm Beach Inn. This was a delightful, typical Lakeshore Hotel just north of Fort Johnston, (now called Mangotchi), long low bungalows each with its own khonde literally on the Lakeshore. The dining room and bar opened directly onto the beach. The Lake itself is about three hundred and fifty miles long and is one of the largest Lakes in Africa. Fringed with palm trees and teeming with a beautiful fish, actually called tilapia melano-pleura or Mossambica, but known in Chinyanja as "Chambo" and a world-wide delicacy. The Lake shore Hotels, of which there were then about five, spread along the Lake, all served this as a speciality, for breakfast, lunch and dinner. Forty six years later I was amazed to find this fish, imported from Zimbabwe, on sale in French supermarkets! I can highly recommend it to anybody who has not tried it!

There were many hippo in the Lake and still quite a few crocodiles. More of these later. A lot of commercial organisations and private individuals owned cottages on the Lakeshore and it was a great place to relax for a weekend. Much longer used to bore me but people did holiday there and it is still promoted by world-wide tourism. What they don't tell you now is that it is advisable to take your own blood supply in case you are in vehicle accident. The incidence of AIDS is now so high in Malawi that to receive local blood is a virtual invitation to becoming HIV positive!

Transport on the Lake was by way of a steamer named the "M.V. Ilala", a well know name in Nyasaland. She was launched in 1951 and remains the main ship on the Lake to this day. Travelling on this one could easily expect Humphrey Bogart to appear on deck. It was like being in another age. The ship made its calls along the Lakeshore, picking up passengers and freight, being greeted as it arrived by hordes of Africans offering goods for sale.

It started its northern passage about thirty miles from Palm Beach at a

'Empire' Class flying boat

place called Monkey Bay, where it had proper moorings and servicing facilities. It was operated by the Nyasaland Railways. The next spot above Monkey Bay was an utterly delightful little paradise called Cape Maclear. There were crystal clear bays with massive underwater rocks, with an absolute profusion of tropical fish, where skin, or later Scuba diving was very popular. Cape Maclear's other claim to fame was that when Southern Africa was served by Imperial Airways their "Empire" Class Flying Boats, used Cape Maclear as a staging point. It must have been a sight to see those huge Flying Boats coming down on the Lake. Goodness knows what the locals thought of them!

The Lake is up to fifty miles wide and usually across the other side can be seen the Mountains of P.E.A., (Mozambique). It was, and no doubt still is, a very, very beautiful place!

Just before I left Zomba the time drew near for Supt. Yorke's UK Leave and he was nominated to attend the Senior Officers' course at Ryton. I have probably given the impression that he was a "blimpish" kind of chap and I hold to that description. A few years later when I was Commissioned, he was Second-in-Command of the Division in Blantyre and the day after my Commission was Gazetted, I had occasion to speak to him on the telephone from Chikwawa, then my Station. I felt sure he would comment on my promotion but nothing. Then just as we were terminating our business, he cleared his throat and said, "Er – Bean. Congratulations". And put the phone down!

M.V. Ilala

So there he was, just about off to Ryton and he said that he wanted of photo of, "His men" to show to his fellow course mates there. It was the rainy season and we waited for days for it to stop raining so that the photo could be taken. Eventually it stopped for half-a-day and the entire PMF was sent off quickly to quarters to dress in No.1 Gear. They were lined up in rows about five deep, standing on benches and stools in front of the MT Garages with the highly polished riot vehicles behind them. The Force Photographer was detailed to take the shots. This was Mike Tadman with whom I messed. A very nice single chap with no previous Police experience but very "Arty-Crafty". A series of shots was taken of "Supt. Yorke with his men" and Tadman was instructed to develop and print enlargements and post them off to England so that, "I can show them to my fellow officers!". The following day off he went to England and Ryton.

The Police Camp meanwhile was in an uproar of hilarity because when Tadman developed the negatives, he had a superb series of shots of the MT Garage roofs! Not a single one of "Me and my men". What to do? The moment could not be reproduced so Tadman waited until Yorke started bleating from UK for his photos and told him they had been sent, together with the negatives, ages ago. They must have been lost in the post between Nyasaland and England as far as Yorke was concerned. This was a not infrequent happening anyway. I never heard the final outcome when Yorke returned from England as I had left Zomba by then.

Tadman did the same thing when my good friend Allan Dew was married. All the wedding shots were of the ceiling in a corner of the room. I still say though that on occasion he was a very good photographer!

Chapter Ten

Mlanje

In February, having completed my three months or so in the PMF, I was posted to Mlanje.

That was probably the easiest move I ever made because at that stage of my life I had accumulated nothing. All I had was my clothing and the faithful Zebio. Before actually going to Mlanje, I had to stop over in Blantyre for three days and do a course in Immigration. I learned that the reason for this was that Mlanje was situated on the border with Portuguese East Africa, adjacent to a Portuguese district called 'Mulanje'. The Police Station at Mlanje also served as the 'Entry Point' in that area for Nyasaland and there was traffic of several hundred Portuguese coming across the border each month to go shopping in Blantyre, fifty miles away. Their entry and departure had to be documented and an extremely boring job it turned out to be. Anyway, the head of the Immigration Service was a half-Portuguese Superintendent seconded from the Police and named John D'Oliveira. He took me under his wing, baffled me with documentation and sent me on my way to Mlanje.

Mlanje Mountain
(From Wikipedia)

Mt. Mlanje is a large monadnock in Southern Malawi with the Town of the same name at its base. Rising sharply from the surrounding plains of Chiradzulu, and is a Tea-Growing area. It measures approximately 13x16 miles (22x26 kilometres) and has a maximum elevation of 3,002m at its highest point, Sapitwa Peak.

Much of the Massif consists of rolling Grassland at elevations of 1800 - 2200m, intersected by deep Forested ravines. It has many individual peaks reaching heights of over 2500m, including Chambe Peak, the West Face of which is the longest rock climb in Africa.

The first European to report seeing the Massif was David Livingstone in 1859. The elevation of the Mountain is high enough for it to disturb upper level air flow and induce rain clouds to form around it, making it an important source of rain water at the head of almost every river that runs through this part of the Country.

Mlanje is actually the name of a beautiful Mountain Range about forty miles long and extending into PEA, hence their name of 'Mulanje'. The peak of the Mountain is over eleven thousand feet high and was reputed to be the third highest mountain in Africa. There was a series of plateaux running along at about eight thousand feet and each one had many paths leading up it. The lowest, and the one nearest our habitation was called Lichenya and I was to know this plateau like the back of my hand. The Government Administrative Area, called throughout East and Central Africa, the "Boma", (literally a fenced in area), was situated on the lower slopes of the mountain at about four and a half thousand feet above sea level. The houses of the officials there were along a track which lead upwards and the more senior the official, the higher his house. Thus the top house was that of the District Commission and the next one down was that of the Officer-in-Charge of Police. They were proper large Colonial type houses but lowly new Inspectors of Police occupied rondavels at the lower end of the road. Every house had a magnificent view across the Palombe plain towards PEA and even the rondavels were comfortable, well maintained and furnished by the Public Works Dept. (PWD).

Mlanje was a fairly large Boma having a District Commissioner, two Assistant District Commissioners, (ADCs), three Police Officers and about seventy black Police. There was also a Doctor, who was to figure quite largely in my life there, a PWD (Works) Inspector, a PWD (Roads) Inspector, an Inspector of Schools, a Post Officer Engineer and they all formed a small community living on the slopes of the mountain. Most were married and had children who were taught locally until they reached proper school age and then went either to boarding school in Blantyre or Rhodesia or even to South Africa or England. All of these officials were white and most of them had a University Degree. The Boma was a predominantly white enclave presided over by the DC, at that time in our case, one Stonehewer Edward Illingworth, (known for some reason as "Sinbad"), who was cricket mad and had a very beautiful wife, Helen. More of Sinbad later! Not of his wife unfortunately.

There was a small Indian trading centre about two miles from the Boma which catered for all our requirements. This included a garage which serviced our cars and sold petrol. The two main store owners were called Kharbari and Patel but they did not socialise with the whites. The District as a whole was not large compared with many others in Nyasaland but was very heavily populated. The local people were of a tribe called the 'Alomwe'

Mlanje Mountain with the tea plantations in the foreground

and were much despised by the other tribes in the country, mainly 'Nyanjas', 'Yaos', 'Angoni' and a few 'Shangan' to the east of the country. In those days, quite a lot of them didn't speak the others' languages so interpreters in Court were always a problem. One of the reasons the Alomwe were despised was their inclination to eat anything, cats, dogs, crocodiles, wild cats – such as gennets and civets – and even leopard!

Tea picking

The District was exclusively a tea growing area in common with its neighbour, Cholo. There were dozens of tea estates, each run by a white Manager, or Owner, assisted by anything up to eight or nine Assistant Managers. All white of course. They lived the 'life of Reilly' in huge houses and lived off the estate. You could have a young man of my age, unmarried perhaps, being totally responsible for the welfare and work of up to eight hundred black workers, plus their families. All housed and fed on the estate. These "Tea Assistants" would have certainly, at the least, a houseboy to keep the house clean, a cook and two or more "Garden Boys" to maintain their vast gardens. All paid for by the estate. Some of the larger company owned estates might employ several thousand black workers and ran schools for their employees' children, clinics for their health and a store for their food purchases. These were on top of their basic rations which were part of their pay. The store ran a "Credit Book" for the employees and deducted it from their pay at the end of the month. Tea grows on mountain sides and must have a lot of rain or irrigation. Ten days after a rain, the tea bushes would develop fresh sprouts, called a 'flushing', and these were immediately hand-picked and taken to the estate factory where the leaf was processed. If it rained every day for three months, as could happen in the rainy season, every day was a tenth day and picking was continuous. The pickers, male and female, worked their way along the rows of tea bushes, carrying a large wicker basket on their backs into which they threw the picked leaf over their shoulders. When their baskets were full they carried them to the edge of the field where they were weighed and emptied into a trailer. Each worker had a card on which the weight of his pickings was entered and he was paid on the basis of what his card said he had picked. I grew to know the process intimately and to love the smell of the tea factories.

The social life of the planters and the Government Officials centred around the local Club. Every District had one, ours naturally called "Mlanje Club", and a very grand sociable place it was. A cricket field, a rugby pitch, (no soccer – those people didn't play soccer!), tennis courts, sometimes a squash court, a billiard room with at least two tables, an eighteen-hole golf course with sand greens and of course, a long, long bar. No cash transactions took place and purchases were made by use of a 'Book of Tickets' which were pre-paid. This was to prevent pilferage. Dances and Barbecues, (called Braais – from the South African), were frequent and the big night of the week was Wednesday when there was a film show. The main hall of the Club was set up with rows of wooden folding seats and one of the tea assistants operated a sixteen millimetre projector at the back of the hall. The programme would start with a News Reel, often Pathe or the South African equivalent and the "News" was anything up to six months old! Imagine my surprise after I had been there for a couple of months when one Wednesday night, the News included the latest running of the St. Leger, the previous September so at least five or six months old! When the horses passed the winning post, there was a little Police Officer stationed by the post and I jumped up and shouted, "That's me! That's me!". The News had to be stopped and replayed so everybody could identify me. Fame at last! After that the main film would be shown, with regular breaks to change the reels. A great evening and a welcome break from life in the bush.

There were three white Police Officers at Mlanje, unusual for a bush Station but necessary because of the amount of work. In charge was a Superintendent, Frank Chevallier. A super chap and he and his wife Paddy, who are still close friends of mine, living in Cape Town, over 50 years later. There were two Inspectors at the Station, Allan Dew and myself. Allan and his wife Anne are also still very close friends and they returned to England many years ago. Allan was designated as Investigations Officer and I, as the "new-boy", was Public Prosecutor. I had a staff of about ten, including a black sub-Inspector who rejoiced in the name of Mennas Friten Njowe. Njowe was a lovely man, always ready to help, always with a wide grin on his face and of course, a really necessary aid in my early days as a Prosecutor. I had much to do with him at Mlanje and bumped into him for many years in different Stations around the country. Then there were numerous Sergeants and many Constables who, amongst other duties, functioned as Bugler, Signaller, (we used Single-Sideband radios for communication with other Stations and HQ), drivers, storekeepers, clerks and so on. There were always ten to fifteen Constables out on foot patrol or on bicycles around the District and they went out for a week at a time. They had set villages to visit but were left to their own devices as there was no way of contacting them or knowing where they were exactly at any given time. Allan had a large staff to investigate all crime reported and this included a section of CID. Special Branch fell directly under Frank Chevallier.

When Allan had a case which he thought was ready for prosecution, he would pass the docket to me. I would go through it and decide if I thought there was a chance of a successful prosecution. If so, we would prepare the docket for Court, interview the witnesses to make sure they still had the same story, (they often didn't!), and then set a date for Court. Witness summons would be prepared and signed by the District Commission who ex-Officio was a Magistrate and the Constables in my section would have to go out and serve the summons, often bicycling forty or fifty miles to do it, and often not finding the witness again!

The Resident Magistrate lived in the next Boma, Cholo, and he had a little circuit to follow. These chaps were usually UK Barristers who had also joined the Colonial Service. They were mainly very forbearing and just and had little material with which to work. The Court Houses were often little more than a grass roof over an open area and the Magistrate sat at a table! At that time our Magistrate was called Derek Bolt and he was enormously helpful to me whilst I was learning the ropes. He went on to become a Judge of the Nyasaland High Court. The Solicitor and Attorneys General were mostly drawn from the same ranks although occasionally one would be drafted in from another Colony. There were a few QCs in the country and they were employed as State Counsels. They did the actual prosecutions in the High Court.

The work as a Public Prosecutor was onerous and boring. Witnesses very often failed to turn up or changed their stories once in the box. Almost inevitably the whole proceedings were in Chinyanja and passed through an interpreter. There was a huge responsibility resting on the interpreter because few of the whites in the Court could understand much of what was going on, white tea planters excepted, (they were totally fluent in the language), and could present a witness' statement in any way he wished. As I grew more proficient with my Chinyanja, a prerequisite to promotion, I not infrequently had to interrupt and say to the Magistrate, "Your Honour, that is not what the witness said". Some Magistrates were also capable of doing this. I must say that I never thought the fault was malicious, but resulted from misunderstanding by the interpreter. This situation was complicated by the fact that we quite often got witnesses or accused from other tribes and most of the more proficient interpreters were capable of speaking several local languages as well as English.

Before leaving the subject of language I should mention that later on – several times whilst I was in Bechuanaland – I was called upon to interpret in Court when a Malawian was in the box. As their language was unknown in that Country.

When the case was murder, the proceedings in the Magistrate's Court were a committal hearing and the Prosecutor had to present the evidence to get the accused committed to the High Court. The docket would then have to be sent to State Counsel who would take it on from there. As we had a great many murders in Mlanje, this kept us very busy and we had to be able to prepare the docket to a high degree of accuracy to satisfy State Counsel. In the early days I had a number of dockets sent back with acid instructions to do this or that with them. A big learning curve, as they say, but worth it and eventually State Counsel used to say that murder dockets I sent to them were well prepared and easy to work with. But that was in the future after a lot of practise!

One duty which all three of us officers took in turn, and which was a welcome break was that of 'Estate Patrols'.

Every so often one of us would take a week and visit a number of tea estates. Usually bunched together in one area. We would go out in the morning in one of the vehicles and call on the Manager/Owner of the estate in order to create a "Police Presence", pick up information which might interest Special Branch and receive reports of any other matters of interest which the manager hadn't bothered to report. We would call on five or six estates each day and submit a combined report at the end of the week. One aspect of these patrols bothered me and that was the fact that I didn't, and still don't, drink tea. Once installed in the manager's office however his "Tea Boy" would come in with a tray, immaculately dressed with a crocheted snow-white tray-cloth with beautiful crockery and an ornate tea-pot. I was obliged, out of politeness, to accept often not one, but two cups of tea and I soon realised that whilst I took the first sip, the manager would watch me closely. After a couple of sips he would always say, "How is it? Good hey? Better than they are growing next door – theirs tastes like s★★t doesn't it?" And of course I had to agree and make some suitable comment about the body of the tea and so on. Then I would be taken off for a tour of the factory and watch them actually making tea. And then off to the next estate, all day. I think if I hadn't disliked tea to start off with, I would have hated it by this time! It was good though to get out of the office and visit beautiful estates and plantations on the mountain and meet people whom I only saw once every couple of weeks in the Club.

I have mentioned Sub-Inspector Njowe before and I have a story illustrating a different aspect of our work in the Colonial Police Service. We had reached a stage in the development of the country whereby selected black Officers started being sent overseas for further training. Njowe was selected to go to Hendon Police College. Frank Chevallier, anticipating problems for Njowe, took me to one side and asked me if I would entertain him in my home and teach him table manners and how to use a knife and fork etc. This may sound ludicrous but he naturally ate like all Africans, with his hands and only African food, msima, (Mealie Meal), a little gravy and a small amount of meat. Sweets were unheard of. This was an unheard of request by Frank but I liked Njowe and had no choice anyway. He was very anxious to learn all he could about the English way of life and listened intently. Searching for a subject on which we could discourse I remembered he was an avid soccer player, as most Africans are. I told him that when he was at Hendon he would be able to go and watch Arsenal, or other clubs play. He had heard of them of course and I told him that he would see anything up to a hundred thousand white men all in one place together. Bear in mind that Nyasaland had only about eight thousand whites in total at this time. He digested this thought for a while and then said to me, "Eh Bwana, but where do all these white men have their maize gardens?". He couldn't conceive of a man who didn't have his own maize garden and couldn't understand where one hundred thousand white men could find the land! He went to Hendon, went to Highbury a number of times and did very well on his course. He was one of the very first black Inspectors!

Following on this story about Njowe and his lack of knowledge of the European way of life brings to mind another social event in Mlanje which illustrated even more the issue.

In May 1958 there was considerable excitement locally regarding the upcoming visit of the Governor General of the Federation, Lord Dalhousie. It was, I think, the first General Tour of the Protectorate by the Queen's Representative since the formation of the Federation.

The District Commissioner, "Sinbad" Illingworth organised a grand cocktail party to be held at his house up the mountain and much desired invitations were sent to local persons of prominence, all the Government Officers of course, the leading tea planters and estate owners, the more senior local Indian store owners, namely Kharbari and Patel and, (a complete innovation), the local Chiefs and their Tribal Elders. I actually think in those enlightened times they were called "Native Authorities"! This was unheard of as I mentioned in my story about Njowe. One simply did not invite Africans into one's house! And perhaps for good reason as I will now tell.

The Chiefs and their cohorts arrived a good hour early for the event, most unlikely as it is well known that Africans have little regard for time. They were shown into the area where large tables were set out holding a magnificent buffet. There were of course a couple of bar tables also. The Africans made an immediate beeline for the food and filled their plates, repeatedly. They also climbed in to the beer. I am not too sure about this but I think at that time also they were not allowed to have European type alcohol and had

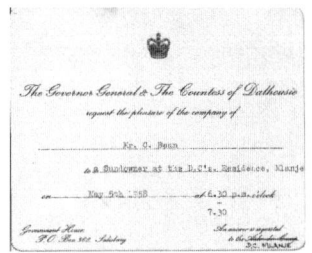

Inspector Bean's invitation to the DC's Cocktail Party in Mlanje

to drink their own Maize Beer and a vile distilled drink called Kachasu which if drunk in sufficient quantities made one go blind!

The Afrikaaners called it "Witblitz", (White lightning!). Anyway, by the time the Governor General and his party arrived, all the food had been eaten, the tables were bare and there was no beer left! And make no mistake, these people were not starving in any way. They simply saw the food was there to be eaten and ate it with no regard for those to follow.

I would imagine that Lord Dalhousie was accustomed to this kind of behaviour as he toured the Federation and in any event people in his position did not, and do not, partake much of refreshment at such functions as they are too busy "Holding Court"!!

An interesting experience though.

Chapter Eleven

The Leopards of Mlanje

Even in those far off days, wild life in profusion was confined to certain areas of Nyasaland. Virtually everywhere had some wild life, but not all varieties. I was fortunate to be stationed in two of the very best areas for game but this was not yet. Mlanje, being a mountain, had an absolute abundance of leopards, hyenas, wild pig, baboon and monkeys – and many, many snakes!

The monkeys, mainly Vervet, were pretty little animals to watch, they were always in our gardens stealing fruit but they created no other problems. The baboon stayed more on the mountain but were a great pest in that they constantly raided the villagers' maize fields and in one night could wreck a field and destroy a family's entire staple diet for the next year. The wild pig, which lived mainly in deep river gorges, very inaccessible, also were deadly for maize fields. They were very dangerous animals to hunt being capable of killing a dog being used to hunt them with ease. Baboon and pig were the main diet of the leopard and were also classified as "Vermin". Any villager killing either had to take the ears into the District Commissioner's Office where they were paid two shillings and sixpence and given an LG shotgun cartridge, shotguns being the means by which they killed the animals. Eventually the villagers would gain the upper hand and the pig and baboon numbers would decrease markedly. This then deprived the leopard of their main diet and they would start marauding the villages looking for the occasional dog, to which they were very partial and any loose goats and sheep. In fact, leopard will eat almost any other animal so nothing was safe.

The villagers would complain to the Government about the number of leopard around and the damage they were doing so the Government would declare leopard also to be "Vermin" and pay a bounty of two pounds ten shillings for any leopard skin brought into the Boma. After a year or two of this, leopard numbers would be diminished and the baboon and pig would increase and become a nuisance again! So the whole cycle would be repeated every few years.

Most of the whites living in the Mlanje area had plenty of experiences with leopard, which of course are very beautiful animals. I think most people living in Mlanje saw a leopard every few weeks and it was not at all uncommon to come home from the Club late at night and find one skulking around the garden in search of pickings, or on occasion even stretched out on the khonde admiring the view. As I have mentioned, the kitchen of most houses, with its wood burning stove, was a rondavel situated just outside the back door and this was the domain of the cook boy. Again, not infrequently a cook boy would be scared half out of his life by a leopard entering the kitchen whilst a meal was being prepared, looking for something to eat.

A leopard incidentally is not really a very big cat, compared to a lion or tiger, and will normally run to about six and a half to seven feet in length from nose to the tip of its tail. A seven foot six leopard is a big animal. They will go to about one hundred and forty pounds for a big one. I mention this because it was not that unusual for an African, somewhere in Nyasaland each year, to kill a leopard with his bare hands in self-defence. The technique, which is instinctive, was to turn sideways to a leopard when it attacked, thus presenting the thigh and hip to the leopard which would usually grip the upper body with its front paws and teeth and rake the lower body of its victim with the rear legs in an attempt to disembowel it.

The victim would try and get his hand down the leopard's throat and choke it from the inside. Of course, if the victim had a spear or a knife in his hand at the time of the attack, his task was made much easier. I may have made this sound a simple procedure but believe me, I have seen a leopard attack twice and the noise and activity is tremendous and ear splitting. A hundred and thirty or forty pounds of snarling spitting fury is terrifying and the reaction is purely instinctive as I have said.

During one of the periods when leopard were on the ascendance, the villagers from one village came into the Police Station to complain that during the night a leopard had entered a hut and taken a dog out from under a blanket also sheltering a child. Had the child been sleeping nearest the door instead of the dog, the leopard would have most likely have taken the child. They wanted action.

What followed was a virtual pantomime. A number of Europeans stationed in the Boma armed themselves with a variety of totally unsuitable weapons and set out to hunt the leopard down. The villagers had tracked it to a small stand of trees not far from the village. I remember, this being my first hunt, I was very excited, and not a little frightened and I carried a huge hunting knife on my belt, my Police .38 Smith and Wesson and an issue .303 rifle. All utterly useless for leopard. A shotgun is the ideal weapon as one only gets a brief sighting usually, in thick bush and at close quarters. Sam Scott, the telephone engineer had a .22 pistol!! The Assistant District Commissioner had a shotgun and the Agricultural Officer had a .303 we loaned to him. A tea assistant named Peter de la Pasture, ex-Kenya and reputed to be also an ex-Big Game Hunter had a double-barrelled shotgun. Off we went to the thicket in which the leopard was holed up and we lined up on one side, spread out about fifty yards apart. The villagers went in from the other side beating drums and saucepans, to drive the leopard out. This they did but it went between them and we never got a chance. This went on all day with the leopard evading us and about mid-afternoon we had what we thought was an ideal situation with the leopard in bush alongside an un-planted maize field. The villagers again went in from the far side and this time the leopard came out towards us. The noise it made was ear shattering and it ran down between furrows on the field so that all we could see was this big fluffed-out tail sticking straight up in the air. I was on top of a huge rock on the edge of the field and could not get a shot. Just off the field in an open area stood Peter de la Pasture, accompanied by the African head clerk from his tea estate. The leopard went straight for him and as it approached he let it have both barrels. Afterwards he swore he saw puffs of dust off the leopard's head where he hit it but had he done so at that range he would have dropped it. We were convinced that in his haste, and fear, he missed at point blank range. On reaching him the leopard stopped, reared up and sank its teeth into his shoulder, gripping him front and rear chest with it's front paws. It did not try and rake him and it was suggested afterwards that this was because it was probably an old animal. Anyway, he was at its mercy having fired both barrels. The head clerk besides him was armed with a bow and a sheaf of arrows held in his hand, again very unsuitable for hunting leopard. However with great bravery and quick thinking he beat the leopard about the head with the bunch of arrows causing it to abandon de la Pasture and make off into the nearest bush. De la Pasture appeared severely wounded, bleeding profusely and we were all very shaken by the suddenness of the event so we called off the hunt for the day and took de la Pasture to the local Hospital. Amazingly, from such a very brief encounter, albeit a very ferocious one, he had one hundred and forty-four puncture wounds in his shoulder, chest and back, all from either bites or claws. A leopard's teeth are full of bacteria as are its claws and he had to have a drain fitted in every hole and it had to be kept open for about a week. He was of course now a subject of fame(?) and I remember, he wore the green shirt he had on at the time of the attack for about two weeks in the Club without washing it. The holes and the blood were the cause of great excitement and he was very proud of them. The head clerk I am pleased to say received a B.E.M. for his bravery. At this stage we realised we were ill equipped both with our armoury and our knowledge, to tackle this leopard so a phone call to the Dept. of Game in Blantyre obtained the services of an experienced hunter the following day.

He was a tall lanky Ranger named Ollie Carey and he arrived the following morning. The villagers had still tracked the leopard and knew where it was holed up again and out we went. I was amazed when we got out of our cars to see that Ollie Carey had brought with him an Alsatian and a Dachshund. He explained that a leopard could always kill a dog, no matter how big, but two dogs together, of whatever size, would put a leopard to flight. The reason being that a leopard cannot stand being harried from two directions and will take to the nearest tree. The day followed much the pattern of the previous day. We would keep finding the leopard, chase it out but never managed to get a shot at it. An interesting point was that Ollie, being a tracker of some skill, showed us time and time again how when we had stopped to have a conference as to what to do, the leopard had circled round, back on its own tracks and had lain some twenty yards or so away from us whilst we had been gathered. About three in the afternoon, the leopard again broke cover and went straight for one of the villagers in its path. As it passed him, it half reared up and swiped the left side of his face with one paw and carried on. The one blow, took off half the villager's face. Ear, eye and cheek. It carried on up the mountain and was never seen again. The villager was taken to the Hospital where his wounds were treated, but he didn't recover and died.

You may remember when I described the living accommodation in Mlanje I mentioned the dirt track, which lead up the mountainside with the houses of the Government Officials set either side of it. The most junior official, at that time - me, being the lowest, and the District Commissioner's relatively "Palatial Residence", together with its swimming pool being the highest. One Sunday afternoon, the Assistant District Commissioner, Brian Walker and his wife were taking an afternoon stroll down the track towards the Boma with their golden cocker spaniel bitch. About fifty yards from my house a leopard suddenly sprang from the bush, seized the spaniel and disappeared back into the bush. All in a second and without a sound being uttered by anything, until Brian's wife screamed! And people today worry about muggers!

I am glad to say that to my knowledge, throughout the whole of Africa, the leopard, which is a magnificent cat, is fully protected. This is not to say that they are not poached for their skins but officially they are protected.

I cannot leave the subject of leopards here without mention of Fred Balestra. Fred was quite an old Yorkshireman who lived round the corner of the mountain on a 'Saddle' called the Fort Lister Gap. He had a lovely old Colonial house and was a kind of farmer, mainly with sheep and a bit of tobacco. This story will raise hairs on people's necks these days but what Fred did was in the name of self-defence and protection of his property. At the time I knew him he had shot one hundred and forty-four leopards, many of them on his lawn and shooting from his bed at night! He had maintained full records of every animal he shot, weight, length, what it was shot with and why it was shot. It was from Fred's records that I know statistics for leopards. One day he phoned me and asked me to go out to his place. His sheep were corralled at night in old tobacco barns which were some forty or fifty feet high with only one doorway and vents very high up. Inside there were cross-beams from which curing tobacco had been hung. A leopard had gained access to one of his barns by climbing a tree next to it and entering through one of the vents. There were a hundred or so sheep in the barn and the leopard killed, in a few minutes, some forty-seven of them. Fred told me that the leopard is the only animal which kills for pleasure as well as for food given the opportunity. It develops a blood lust and kills and kills until there is nothing left to kill. They only take what they want to eat. Fred had disturbed the leopard on hearing the noise the killing made, entered the barn and shot the leopard. After seeing the mayhem entailed, I understood why he shot leopards on sight!

The Fort Lister Gap where Fred Balestra lived was a 'Saddle' halfway up the mountain, looking out to the east over Portuguese East Africa, (PEA), and to the west across the Palombe Plain towards Zomba Mountain. At the foot of the mountain was quite a large settlement, Palombwe, of mainly the Alomwe and it had a very large market. When visiting the area I was often amazed at the number of Africans I would see with the bottom half of their legs missing, or perhaps the lower portion of an arm. Also there were hideous disfigurements whereby the person had half of his face missing. On enquiry I found that this was all due to attacks by hyenas. Palombe was home to reputedly the only place in Africa inhabited by man-eating hyenas. Hyenas are very large dog-like creatures, very ugly and appearing to be deformed by their huge forequarters sloping away rapidly to relatively very small hindquarters. They have enormously powerful necks and jaws and can crack the marrow bone of a giraffe. They are the only animals capable of cracking a human skull, with their jaws. They are often hermaphrodite, possessing the genitals of both sexes and are generally regarded as scavengers. In fact they are, but are very capable of hunting and killing their own prey. Palombe, being down on the plain, is an intensely hot place and in the summer season the villagers were accustomed to sleeping on their khondes under the eaves of their huts. The hungry scavenging hyenas found them easy meat, to coin

a phrase, and would dart in whilst the villagers were sleeping and grab the nearest available piece of meat, hence the loss of so many limbs or faces. Sometimes a number of hyenas, or "mfisi" as they were known, would attack the same man and they were then able to make off with the whole meal, as it were. The rest of the village would lie quaking in their beds listening to their fellow, often a relative, being dragged

off by the mfisi, screaming and, it seemed to me, to be crying the obvious complaint, "Mai mai, ndi mfa". Literally, "Mother mother, I am dying!". Eventually the screams would terminate and the villagers would then go back to sleep, coming in to the Police Station the following morning to report the death. I went out many times to these scenes and it was gruesome indeed following the trail of the pack of mfisi, picking up the odd piece of bone or flesh missed by the mfisi until the trail petered out and they had eaten the whole of the victim. Our Government Doctor, about whom more later, used to declare death merely on the presence of a few pieces of bone! Hyenas were considered "Vermin" by the Government all the time I was in Nyasaland and as was the case with other Vermin, the Boma paid a bounty for each one killed. A final note on hyenas at this stage is to mention that they are generally regarded throughout much of Africa as somewhat mystical animals.

They are thought to be the familiars of witches whom it is believed ride around on their backs at full moon!

Chapter Twelve

Typical Mlanje Crime

Crime at Mlanje fell into two main categories. These were crimes against the person and crimes against property. Housebreaking and burglaries were very common and very easy to perpetrate as virtually the entire population lived in what were called "pole and dagga" huts. These are very common throughout Africa and are constructed by building a wooden framework from, usually wattle poles and then plastering it with one form

Typical African hut

of mud or another. The whole thing was then thatched with grass – very flammable grass! The actual shape of the hut varies considerably throughout the continent but in Nyasaland they were almost always circular. Some tribes in other parts of Africa decorated their huts very attractively but the Nyasas did not. There was only one entrance usually closed by a grass, or occasionally a wooden door and there were no windows. Cooking was done on an open fire outside the door and in the winter season, it was quite common to build a fire actually inside the hut to keep the occupants warm.

Whole families would sleep in the one hut which had no divisions inside and of course, with a fire added under the thatched roof, death by burning was very frequent. It was also extremely easy to gain illegal entry into the hut during the family's absence and we often had reports of an entire hut being cleaned out, of pitiful belongings because they had no furniture to speak of, a couple of chairs and chests and sometimes wooden beds strung with leather thonging. So what was stolen was clothing and money, making detection difficult, the clothing all being very similar and money unidentifiable.

Our clear-up rate on thefts and break-ins was not very good but we did try. A word here about the interrogation techniques of the African Detectives. I found that by our standards they were incredibly hard on their fellows, physically. I could not however fail to laugh when one day, in a neighbouring office I heard the sounds of blows and heard one of the Detectives, himself as black as the ace of spades, calling a suspect a "black bastard!". This was standard procedure although of course we tried to stop it. They never seemed to learn that beating prisoners did not obtain information. The suspects kept totally silent and almost never revealed information.

The prize for this kind of treatment though has to go to one of our Detective Sergeants named Barton Perenje. Perenje was very well thought of in the Force and was going places. One day he brought a prisoner suspected of housebreaking to my office. The chap was dressed in a pair of shorts, "kabadula" they were called, and a filthy shirt. I should mention as this is germane to the story that this was before the days of fly zips. Perenje said to me, "This man has a complaint Bwana". I did not speak Chinyanja well at that stage and Perenje had to translate for me. I asked the man what his complaint was and Perenje translated his answer, "I have been assaulted Sir". I asked by whom and got the reply, "By a certain person". (It was always a "certain person" who did something, not somebody or a name). Patiently I asked who the person was and back came the reply through Perenje, "By myself Sir!". I asked Perenje what was the nature of the assault and he spoke to the suspect who thereupon undid the buttons of his shorts and pulled out his penis, looking something like a foot of black pudding. Through his foreskin was fastened (!) a safety pin of the size and type we would call a kilt pin. I said, "Did you do that Sergeant?", and he said, "Yes Sah". I asked him why and he said, "Because the prisoner will not reveal where the stolen property is!". I told him to take the pin out at once and not to do it again. He looked at me as if I were crazy, bent down, removed the pin from the chap's foreskin and without more ado, carefully put it through the lapel of his jacket, no doubt for use with the next prisoner who would not, "reveal where the property is!"

The sequel to this story is that about an hour afterwards, when it was clear to me that the suspect was not going to have it, I ordered his release. The next morning the Headman from the village concerned came into the Police Station and said that the released suspect had run away in the night but all the stolen property had been left at the door of the house where it had been stolen! I pondered that there was perhaps justification for Perenje's success!

There were many suicides, invariably by hanging, either from a tree or from the beams of the hut where the deceased had lived. Since the beams were not much more than strong poles, and only six or seven feet above the ground, to kill himself, (and they were almost always males), the perpetrator had to tie a rope or something round one of the barely overhead poles, then round his neck, then bend his legs until he lost consciousness and choked to death. You really have to want to die to go to those lengths! Other than drunkenness we didn't often find a reason for the suicide.

Fights usually broke out over a woman or more often after bouts of drinking, the liquor being maize beer, of which a great deal has to be drunk before intoxication takes place, or last of all "Kachasu". This was a very potent, evil, foul smelling liquor made by distilling beer, or anything else which was handy. To it would often be added anything which might "hep" it up. Meths was ideal, (that blindness finally resulted from drinking this was of no moment), surgical spirit, old spirits or anything which might make it "go off!". So this was 'Kachasu' and it was illegal. In South Africa it is called "Skokiaan", or from the Afrikaans, "Witblitz", which translates as "White Lightning!" Very apt!

Once through the sound barrier on this kind of stuff anything was possible and the injuries resulting from fights were heinous indeed. They would pick up the nearest object and let fly with it. If it was a knife, a spear or an axe death frequently resulted.

Assaults however were not totally confined to being committed under the influence. One of the most bizarre murders I had to deal with at Mlanje occurred when a man had a puncture to his bicycle tyre on the road from Palombe. A passer-by, unknown to the cyclist, watched him mending the puncture and taunted him for getting one. He ended up by calling the cyclist, "Ncence inu!". Translated as, "You fly!". The cyclist picked up a spanner he was using to fix his bike and crashed it onto the other man's head, repeatedly, until he was dead. It transpired when I enquired that to call somebody a "Fly" in Chinyanja was a great insult since flies eat excrement! Not, I would have thought, sufficient an insult as to warrant getting your head smashed in!

With all these murders, suicides and accidental deaths we used to average about four sudden deaths a week at Mlanje, each requiring a Post Mortem examination which had to be attended by one of the senior Officers, as the junior one there, this fell to my lot for a year or more. I can truthfully say that I saw more forms of death in Mlanje than most UK Police Officers could ever imagine. In fact I challenge anybody to tell me of a form of death I have not seen!

To digress a moment and to encompass my total African Police Service, I have seen death by being eaten by lion, leopard and hyena. By being trampled by elephant and buffalo, by being bitten in half by hippo, by being taken and drowned by crocodiles. By being stabbed or beaten with spears, arrows, knobkerries, knives etc. By being struck by lightning, electrocuted accidentally and drowning. By being shot by a variety of firearms, by being killed in dynamite explosions, by Judicial Hanging, (of which more later). By poisoning, usually during witchcraft proceedings or accidentally. By falling off mountain-tops or down mine shafts. I attended a dozen or more Exhumations, some from very recent burials, some not so recent. Absolutely vile. You name it, I've been there, and done that!!

Back to Mlanje and a few words about our Medical Officers. Most Districts or Bomas, had an expatriate Doctor in charge of the Hospital and taking care of our health. Some of them were very good, some of them were awful. One of their unenviable tasks was carrying out the Post Mortems, (PMs as they were called), previous referred to. If he was very busy, we would store up the bodies for a few days, only a few days though because of the heat and with no refrigeration, then spend an entire afternoon doing five or six PMs. They were not often very complicated since the cause of death was usually very apparent. I attended so many that I could certainly have carried out one myself and with experience found that I could be of considerable help often with suggestions as to what to look for.

As most Policemen and Nurses and Doctors will know, to cope with the unpleasant side of life such as death so often, we develop a macabre sense of humour, probably as a form of defence. PMs were rarely quiet sombre occasions which they really should be.

One Irish Doctor, whom I will obviously not name, took the biscuit for bizarre behaviour however. I have mentioned the many deaths by burning we had and usually the victims were burned to a cinder and curled up in what is called the "typical pugilistic attitude". We had one of these in and for some reason this particular Doctor carried out the PM by himself. This chap was quite eccentric, and carried out his PMs, sensibly for that climate, in his underpants, white theatre Wellington boots, and a big green rubber apron and huge heavy red rubber gloves. He looked quite a sight in operation I can tell you!

Following this PM where I wasn't present, he told me that the body was not charred at all but was just "cooked to a 'T'!" As he was alone, he could not resist taking a thin slice off the buttock and tasting it!! Just for the experience! Knowing the man I could only believe him. Obviously we never spoke of it to anybody else and I was eternally grateful that I had not attended this one or I might have been invited to participate!

Witchcraft was in these days rife throughout Africa, and believe it or not, it still is a major force, even in the cities today. Most natural disasters such as cattle dying, crops failing, unexplained deaths, no rain, too much rain and so on were frequently laid at the doors of local villagers who were disliked for some reason or who were believed to have gained by the disaster. It was normal practice to call in the services of a "Sangoma", a Witchdoctor to smell out the witch. These Sangomas were much feared and often were very powerful. They were credited with wonderful "powers" but in fact used a form of "Trial by Ordeal" to smell out the witch. One form of trial was simply to dance about waving "Magic Wands", hyena tails and so on in front of the assembled village until the guilty person's nerve broke and they ran away or confessed. Another less pleasant form was to boil a small, special pot of water and sit the person suspected on the pot with their genitals in the boiling water. If they were guilty, their private parts were terribly damaged. If they were innocent, no harm came to them!!! Guess how many times the witchdoctors were wrong!

In Africa there are many different forms of "Trial by Ordeal", often involving poison. In Nyasaland there is a tree called the 'Mwabvi' tree. When its bark is stripped off and boiled, the resultant brew is very, very potent and lethal if taken in the correct dosage. The suspected witch was made to drink from a cup of the Mwabvi and if he threw up, he was innocent. If he was very ill, or died, he was guilty. The belief amongst those who studied witchcraft was that the man who knew he was innocent would take a hearty swig at the cup, believing that his innocence would protect him. The massive ingestion produced vomiting and all the poison came back. The man who knew he was guilty took only a small swallow and this induced considerable illness or even death. People who were thus "proved" to be witches were put to death by the villagers, perhaps by being stoned, thrown off a cliff or being burned at the stake. I had two such cases during my service on the Lower River as you will read later on.

Our Resident Magistrate in Mlanje was a very nice chap called David Bolt whom I have mentioned before. He was very nearly killed by Mwabvi when he tried a witchdoctor and found him guilty. The witchdoctor "cursed" him from the dock and told David he would die before the day was out. The witchdoctor was hustled out of Court and sent down and later in the day David was taken violently ill. For two days he hovered at death's door and all the locals were greatly impressed by the witchdoctor, who had he been free, could have increased his fees greatly. After heavy treatment involving stomach pumping etc. David Bolt recovered. His stock of course also increased greatly since he had proved that his witchcraft was even stronger than the witchdoctor's! Our Doctors believed that in handling the exhibit of a pot of Mwabvi, David Bolt had taken a small amount into his system. He often sat at the bench with the heel of his hand around his mouth, considering evidence and this must have been how he got the Mwabvi into his system. Throughout my entire career in the Colonial Police I dealt with many cases of witchcraft and am certain it still continues throughout the Continent.

Chapter Thirteen

Mlanje Mountain

As I have mentioned previously, Mlanje, as it was known, (without the "Mountain" suffix), was a very beautiful, albeit very hot place to live. It was in fact a range about forty miles long. If my memory serves me well, it comprises about seven plateaux. Each joined to the next and with many, many paths up to each plateau.

Countless streams flowed down the mountainside, the vegetation of which was dense tropical bush, abounding with snakes of many kind, baboons, monkeys, wild pigs and leopard together with an endless variety of bird life.

The plateaux were composed of vast rolling grasslands and a lot of pine plantations which caused the whole mountain to be administered by the Forestry Department. The local Forestry Officer was a nice chap named Geoff Ayers and he was built like a greyhound. He was up and down the mountain all-day and seemed to be tireless. Although I was nothing like as fit as he was, I was only twenty-two and also very fit and most weekends found me up the mountain, one day, even in-between playing rugby and water polo! One of the attractions up the mountain, apart from the very noticeable drop in temperature owing to the height, was the fact that the little streams abounded in trout – albeit very small trout. The streams were too small and too crowded for the fish to grow anything much bigger than six inches and they were quite unsophisticated as trout go. Officially fishing required a Permit and 'Fly' only was allowed. However, being the local Policeman, nobody was going to ask me for a licence or check on what I was using to fish. In any event, it was a most rare occurrence to see anybody up there. So my friend Les Renno and I used to sneak up armed with little fibreglass bream rods and with our hats dutifully carrying a small display of flies, and in our back packs, a big tin of worms, a pound of butter, salt, a little gas burner and a copper bottomed frying pan. The trout thought Christmas had come with these big fat worms

The old DC's house with Mlanje Mountain in the background

being dangled in front of them and we would quickly catch about six, head and tail them and clean them, into the frying pan in butter, barely cook them, eat them, wash them down with beautiful clean mountain water and move on to the next pool where we repeated the operation. The streams were rarely more then fifteen feet or so across and a couple of feet deep. Without doubt, I have never tasted such superb fish in my life. Freshly caught, minutes before, young and tender – and poached. They say poached meat always tastes the best! After a morning up there we would make our way down, exercised, fed and happy!

Because I went up the mountain so much, I knew my own part very, very well. The climb to the plateau level of Lichenya took about three hours depending on the fitness of the party and visitors to Blantyre, expressing a desire to climb the mountain were often referred to the Policeman in Mlanje who was always up the mountain – Me!! I often took people up with me but the most interesting party I took up was a Film Crew, making a documentary for television, on the journeys of David Livingstone. He of course had been to Mlanje, he had been everywhere it seemed and had indeed been up Mlanje. The expedition was lead by one Quentin Keynes, a film producer and the son

He Followed Zambesi Trail Of Dr. Livingstone

Newspaper cutting of the Mlanje Expedition

of Admiral Sir Geoffrey Keynes, a Naval Surgeon. He was accompanied by an American Olympic Swimmer named Dave Coughlin and Sir Laurence Olivier's son Tarquin. How they came to be involved with Keynes I never learned. They asked me if I would employ about twenty porters to carry all their film equipment and take them up the mountain. I readily agreed to this and they came to stay in my house for about a week whilst the trip was put together. I must say that leading this long line of porters with heavy loads on their heads and the three white men up the mountain, I felt quite like David Livingstone myself! Dave Coughlin being a swimmer and Tarquin Olivier being a rowing man were very fit and had no trouble with the climb. They enjoyed themselves immensely but Quentin Keynes, although in his early thirties was very unfit and moaned and complained from the outset. They got their films of, and from, the top of the mountain and in the late afternoon we set off down. Quentin by this time was very tired and slow and we went ahead leaving him to make his own way down with a couple of the porters, who both knew the mountain well. Unfortunately it got so dark even the porters lost their way and by late evening we were starting to think about search parties when Quentin Keynes and the porters staggered out of the darkness in the District Commissioner's garden, his being the highest house on the mountain and therefore the only visible lights at that time. Quentin had twisted his ankle badly and had to stay another two days before he was fit enough to move but off they went having had a successful trip up Mlanje.

Each of them afterwards wrote me very nice letters of thanks which I still have.

120 Regents Park Road, London NW1

October 30th 1958

Dear Chris,

You probably think of me as a real bastard for not having written you since we left Mlanje. Well, you know, I'm not really! I have not written to anyone during this expedition of mine - and this includes my poor parents and girl -friend! You see, it's damned difficult setting pen to paper, or rather, typewriter to paper in my case, when you' re driving all day, tired at night, and the next day's the same........

So I resolved that I wasn't going to write to anyone until I got on-board ship to return to the UK. And so now, here I am, nearing the White Cliffs of Dover – or something similar – and getting down to writing everyone – which includes Police Inspector Bean!

You certainly were damned good to the three of us while under your roof and charge – and, looking back on it, this even includes our fateful trip up Dear old Mlanje.

Do you know our escapade up that bloody mountain is famous? On this ship I was chatting to another passenger, a complete stranger, and we got onto the subject of Mlanje, and he said to me, " Were you one of the three chaps who came down exhausted in the moonlight from it one night and pitched up at the DC's?". Small world isn't it?

I just hope those photos come out after all the stress and strain! But thanks a million, Inspector, for your hospitality to us and I hope that sometime I can do the same for you in New York, London or Newmarket. Just let me know when you're coming, and I'll bake a cake. You have my address - we must keep in touch. And if I should get up to Dear old Doncaster soon, (and I well may) , I'll be sure to let your folks know how their son is faring.....

All the best. Keep your chin strap on.....

Yours *Frank*

My final claim to fame with regard to Mlanje Mountain was that I believe I was probably the first, and perhaps the last, to take a horse up the mountain. A friend of mine named Mike Ryan who lived on the Palombe Plain imported three or four Basuto Ponies from Basutoland. These ponies, bred in the mountains in Basutoland, are small, sturdy, sure-footed and utterly fearless. I used to go out in the early morning before work and go for a nice cool ride with Mike. One day I asked him if I could borrow one and see if I could get it up the mountain. I should mention that the path up the mountain was very narrow, often very steep and sometimes just composed of big rock steps. He happily agreed thinking perhaps that if it were possible to get a horse up, he might hire them out to visitors who didn't want to expend their own energy climbing Mlanje.

One Sunday morning very early, before the heat got up, I set off up Lichenya aboard my little horse. I was amazed at the animal's confidence on stretches with a sheer drop of hundreds of feet on one side and its willingness on the very steepest stretches. On some difficult sections I had to get off and walk but we managed it and I still believe that I was the first man to ride a horse on top of Mlanje Mountain!

I had to tell Mike though that I didn't think it was a commercial proposition as it was very arduous, not to mention somewhat nerve wrecking!

Chapter Fourteen

Our Portuguese Neighbours

One of the most boring and arduous tasks I had to undertake at Mlanje was the keeping of the Immigration Register. As I have mentioned, the Mlanje/Nyasaland border was contiguous in that area with that of Portuguese East Africa, (now known as Mozambique). The Portuguese Administration of its Overseas Territories was very interesting in that it was similar to that of the Roman Empire and all of its Dominions were considered an integral part of the Mother Country. So, "P.E.A.", as we knew it, was a part of Metropolitan Portugal and treated as just another Province. The inhabitants of the country were all considered to be Portuguese Citizens and there was very definitely no colour bar. Instead there existed what one might call a "Culture Barrier". Persons of whatever colour could aspire to any position in the country. The blacks could attain all the privilege of the white citizen by meeting certain cultural requirements, which included education, assets etc., and they then became what were called "Assimilados". At a time when it was virtually unheard of almost anywhere in Africa to see a black sitting in a bar with white people, it was quite common in PEA – a place where traditionally the white Portuguese were very harsh to their blacks.

A District such as Mulanje, our neighbouring District, was run by a very senior Government Official, called an 'Administrador', similar in function to our District Commissioner but with far greater powers. In fact the power of life or death. He had a very large Administrative Staff assisting him and it was interesting to see the type of people they were. The more senior positions were held by what you might almost call "Aristocratic" types, usually good looking, well spoken, most of them speaking English, well dressed and well paid. The junior positions were held by what you might call "Peasant" types. These people looked facially different, dressed much more poorly and didn't have a lot of money. The same could be said of the staff of the tea estates, of which there were many because obviously, sitting on the same mountain with the same climate as Mlanje, the main, in fact the only crop, was tea again. The managers of these estates and their senior staff were also of the more "Aristocratic" type and their tea assistants were little more than "Peasants".

I mentioned that the Portuguese were hard on their blacks and in fact they made our Sgt. Perenje look like a nursemaid. As a punishment, or as a form of interrogation, they used what was called a Bastinado. This was something like a table tennis bat, made of hard heavy wood, and with large holes drilled through it. When used as punishment, the miscreant was made to hold out his hands one by one, and so many strokes were administered. Apart from the immediate pain, the after-effects of the holes were to make the hands swell up to three or four times their usual thickness. For more serious punishment or interrogation, the recipient was made to lie on his back on the floor and his feet were lashed to a pole which was held in the air at about waist level. Then the Bastinado was applied to the soles of his feet! Walking was impossible after this treatment for some time, but recovery from it was fairly rapid and there was no lasting damage. But the recipient would remember it all right and think twice about doing whatever he had done again. As I said, the Administrador also had the power of the death sentence for serious crimes such as murder.

Our nearest Seaside was a place on the Indian Ocean called Quelimane, or a smaller place called Pebane. Occasionally a group of us would set off for a long weekend at the Seaside to get away from the heat of Mlanje. The trip was about five hours in good weather but I remember one trip in the rainy season when we reached a place where there was about two hundred yards of road completely washed away and churned up by heavy lorries. The result was a muddy quagmire literally about three feet deep in soft mud. No problem for the Portuguese. They simply pressed into service several hundred of the local villagers and had them on standby at each end of the muddy stretch of road. When a car came along, twenty or thirty, perhaps more, of these villagers would approach the car, with the occupants still in it and pick it up and literally carry it through the mud to the far side and deposit it on firm ground again. Never underestimate the strength of manpower. If you have enough hands, you can move anything!

To get back to the arduous task I started this section with. Mlanje was the Port of Entry for the Portuguese to come into the country and this they did with great frequency many times a month. Their purpose in visiting was to go shopping in Blantyre which seemed to them almost a shopping paradise with its two or three supermarkets, or "Self-Service" shops as we called them then. They had to complete an entry form at our office, unfortunately only printed in English(!) and we had to stamp their Passports stating how long they were allowed to stay. On their departure, usually the same day, the procedure was reversed. The contents of the form then had to be transferred to our Immigration Register, all by hand remember! At the end of the month a return had to be submitted to Immigration Headquarters in Blantyre. This did not consist simply of numbers but included the names and passport details of every entrance and departure. Since there were often several hundred of these, particularly at some times of the year, it could take me several evenings at home by the light of a paraffin lamp. It was for this I was sent on the course at Immigration HQ with John D'Oliveira. It was a very hard job to do especially dealing with unfamiliar names and one would hope that in Blantyre, the lists were checked off with some Master Register to see who was coming in and out of the country and if we wanted them. All in all a fairly vacuous operation.

We made friends with some of the more senior Portuguese estate people and were invited over for a day or an evening meal. These were always staggering in their sumptuousness and the way they lived just about blew our minds.

A knowledge of Portuguese would have helped the immigration job and one colleague we had, Les Acton, (known as "Tea-Pot" because of his protruding ears), was especially conscientious in his approach to this problem. The Portuguese were almost entirely Catholic and so was Acton. He realised that their Catechism and the English one were identical translations. He obtained a Portuguese one and working with his own, learned a very passable and working knowledge of Portuguese.

It sometimes came in very helpful.

Chapter Fifteen

Africanisms!

A couple more reminiscences of Mlanje. I was in the Boma one day when I heard the most awful screaming outside. I saw something I had never seen before nor have since. A swarm of bees had descended on an African walking by and stayed on him. He disappeared completely under what must have been thousands of bees all stinging him. He was covered with a blanket and the bees were hosed off him and he was taken to the Hospital. He died very quickly from what must have been a massive mass-injection of venom. The PM on him didn't take long!!

Another thing I had to become accustomed to at Mlanje was the African pronunciation, usage and writing of certain English words. It was often very funny. As to usage, if they were referring to somebody who travelled around a lot they would say he was "Too movious!". If they were going to visit somebody they would say they were going for a "Jolly walk".

They always referred to us as "their Fathers", there to teach them. I remember a super chap, Sgt. Mlaviwa saying to me one day, "But Sir, you are here to help us. We are but savages!!!" That could make you think a bit about the responsibility you really carried.

This paternity story could sometimes place one in a very invidious position. At one of my later Stations I had a Radio Operator named Msongwe. He was a bit of a waster and was always up on some kind of charge in front of me. I lost sight of him due to my transfers however but many years later, after I had left the Police, I drove with one of my then colleagues, Jock Forbes, into the yard behind Divisional Police HQ in Mzuzu in the far north of Malawi, as it had by then become. A group of Constables standing in one corner chatting broke up on our arrival and after we got out of the car, one of them ran up to us saying, "Oh, oh, it is my 'Fether' (Father). Hello Deddie!". It was the infamous Msongwe! I was horrified, and of course the story was taken back to Bulawayo by Jock and trotted round the office! Thank goodness the chap was clearly a pure black!

Mlaviwa one day carried out an inventory check on the riot store for me. On his completed list there were a number of items I could make neither head nor tail of and one was "50 Lace pratas" written thus. I puzzled over this for some time and then sent him to fetch me a "Lace prata". They turned out to be respirators for use with tear gas. The letters "L" and "R" are totally interchangeable in many African languages because they usually cannot say an "R". Understanding this, a respirator can easily become a "Lace prata". Thus a Carrot would be a "Kaloti", they usually end words with a vowel.

I almost failed my first oral Chinyanja Examination, very necessary for promotion, because I could not translate the word "Chalici". Very simply, a Church! "C" is almost always said as "Ch" as well. Once you get the hang of this pronunciation it becomes natural and in fact if you don't know the Chinyanja word for something, often saying it phonetically as above will get you through. The final story on language though is in my opinion the best.

In spite of quite proper training in the Police Depot, the investigation methods of our junior staff were often rough and ready and when a complainant came into the Charge Office to make a complaint, the receiving Constable would often make a preliminary enquiry on the spot. So, when a girl came in to complain that she had been raped, as well as taking a statement, the Constable on duty would sometimes even make a preliminary medical examination! I know, the mind boggles! Anyway, in this one instance, this happened, and when the Constable submitted his initial report of the complaint, he wrote in his report, "I examined the complainant and found traces of space men on her abdomen!" I ask you – Extraterrestrials in Mlanje? When I got him in and sorted it out, he had found a specimen, (hence space man), of semen, on her abdomen. Imagine trying to get that one through Court!!

Chapter Sixteen

The State of Emergency

The Federation of Rhodesia and Nyasaland was formed in 1953 by the joining together of Northern Rhodesia, (now Zambia), Southern Rhodesia, (now Zimbabwe) and Nyasaland, (now Malawi). The reason for the creation of the Federation was mainly Political although there were certain Economic justifications. Southern Rhodesia was by far the most developed, and wealthiest, and had in fact been offered Independence as far back as 1923. The Government of the day opted to remain a Self-Governing Dominion with a Governor General, in my time, Lord Dalhousie, representing the Queen. This decision was bitterly regretted in later years. Northern Rhodesia was rich in Copper and a welcome addition to the triumvirate. Nyasaland had very little except manpower to offer. It produced tea, tobacco, coffee and groundnuts and that was it.

The African National Congress, long a Political Body in South Africa had similar parties in the three Territories, none of them very active. There were minor rebellions in 1953 but these were soon put to rest and peace reigned for another three or four years.

In 1958 there returned to Nyasaland, (the country of his birth), one Dr. Hastings "Kamuzu" Banda. He was at that time the most highly educated Nyasaland African and had left the country many years ago under the auspices of an American Mission to go to America and pursue his studies. These resulted in him becoming a Medical Doctor and for many years he was in private practice in London. The political movement in Nyasaland, The Nyasaland African Congress, was looking for, at that time, a figurehead Leader, remembered Banda, almost then at retiring age in London, and he was invited to return to the country to become the Leader of the N.A.C. He was intended to be a figurehead and little could anybody then imagine the grip he finally achieved on the country.

His story is long enough to be dealt with separately but let me jump a few years and say that when I left Malawi finally in 1970, he owned personally half of most of the business enterprises in the country, under the guise of 'Press Holdings'. (A thinly disguised play on the word "President!"). Current figures maintain

Dr. Hastings "Kamuzu" banda

that he amassed a fortune in the region of $300m outside the country and this has never been recovered. He was one of Africa's most successful and powerful dictators and was finally toppled from power at the disputed age of ninety-nine years, reputedly senile.

However, back to 1958. There were Political stirrings in all three Territories around this time but I will confine myself to those in Nyasaland. There was an ample supply of people with little else to do but support political aspirations. These people arose in this way.

One of the most laudable desires of all Africans, throughout Africa, is the need for education. They will go to the most extraordinary lengths to obtain education for their children. Unfortunately, having got a certain level of education, they were in fact overeducated for the kind of work available. They obtained what was then called 'Standard Six', about the level of the 11-plus in England and this just about qualified them to obtain employment as a clerk in business. A "Cleck" as they called it. They usually took until the age of eighteen or nineteen to reach this level, (bear in mind they were learning in English, not their own language), and then found that there was a gross oversupply of would-be "Clecks". Having worked very hard to obtain a level of literacy, they were not going to take the work of which there was a plentiful supply, labouring, in the tea plantations or tobacco fields. There was very little Industry in Nyasaland. The infrastructure was simply unable to accommodate these thousands of part-educated Africans and so they sat about on street corners and in their villages, and fermented trouble. They were ideal fuel for the Nationalist Movements and were fed the ideas that if they fought for and obtained Independence, there would be big jobs, big cars, big houses, and most importantly, white wives waiting for them. It became quite common for a white wife to be told by her garden-boy or cook that when Independence came, she would become his wife! This story was repeated ad infinitum throughout Africa. The real reasons for the build-up of troubles in all three Territories was without doubt, a very natural desire to be self-governed and to be able to decide their own fates. They also wanted work and wealth, both of which have never materialised in any of the Independent States since. Again, desires which nobody could deny were very understandable – but unobtainable as far as the latter two were concerned. The countries were too small and the infrastructures too undeveloped, and largely incapable of being developed sufficiently to employ the vast numbers wanting work. This applies to this day, viz. the gigantic "Informal Settlements" as they are called around the major cities in South Africa today. Squatter towns really. These house literally millions of blacks, wanting to work, unable to get it and being reduced to crime to survive.

So, in Nyasaland we started to get Indian stores being burned. Schools and rural hospitals being destroyed. Villagers who refused to join the Party being intimidated and often killed. Cars were being burned and crops destroyed. We would get primitive roadblocks set-up causing great inconvenience and eventually fear amongst the whites. The Police started to come under heavy pressure dealing with the increased levels of crime. Special Branch were very occupied identifying Party officials and checking their movements and activities and I thought the Government, through the Police, were pretty much on top of the situation.

The illegal acts of insurrection started to become alarming and in January 1959 word came of a big political Rally to be held in Blantyre. A number of Officers were called in from out Stations such as Mlanje, to be attached to and command the PMF, (Specially trained for Riot Duties). I was selected to go from Mlanje and here my sins came back to catch me.

You may remember the advice I received from Messrs Graves, Pallister and Burgess before leaving England, i.e. spend your outfit allowance on whatever you want because you will never be asked to account for it. Well, with the instruction to report to Police Headquarters was a list of camping items we were required to bring with us. That is, all the items which were listed on the instructions accompanying the outfit allowance! Major panic ensued on the Station and there was much scurrying around, buying items at the Indian stores, borrowing camping equipment from other government officers who did in fact camp as part of their duties and eventually, I managed to get together all the necessary equipment. Off I went to Zomba with all my gear, never to be asked to use it once! Graves and Co.'s advice still held good!

The day of the Rally came, a Sunday, and off we went in force to Blantyre. There were several hundred of us, black and white Officers and although the rally took place, there was no trouble, no doubt as a result of the considerable Police presence. I had to stand, in full riot gear, at the head of a platoon of PMF, at 'The Clock Tower' in Sclater Avenue in Blantyre, in the blazing sun, for nearly six hours. We were deployed at the foot of the Clock Tower, a famous local landmark in Blantyre and one which still is, (although it has been moved since those days). I have a photograph from the London Illustrated News of that week showing me clearly standing there in the sun, waiting for trouble which didn't come – then!

Eventually we stood down and I returned to Mlanje where things were really hotting up. In the analysis carried out after the Emergency was over, Mlanje was one of three or four real hotspots in the country.

At the time there were only two Officers at Mlanje Police Station, myself and Allan Dew who was acting Officer-in-Charge. Our previous Superintendent, Frank Chevallier, had gone on overseas leave and his replacement had not yet arrived. Allan, who was only a year older than me had a lot on his plate being in

Inspector Bean at the head of his PMF Platoon at the Clock Tower in Blantyre

charge of a fairly large Station with a very large population, a number of who were hell-bent on making our lives miserable. Chief amongst these was one named Horace Chikafa, the local Party Leader. Allan had endless meetings with him, giving, or refusing, permission for meetings and such. He was a big man physically and a very unpleasant man with whom to deal. He was without doubt, at that time, Allan's bete noir. At this time, the Government, or more precisely the Special Branch made what I personally considered to be a big mistake. The country was in a state of smouldering insurrection and looked as if, in some places, Mlanje in particular, it was going to boil over. I was only a lowly Inspector then but I would have thought there existed ample reason to declare a National State of Emergency and put the country under Martial Law. The full forces of law and order could then have been brought into play to quell the uprising. Instead, two Special Branch Officers disclosed the "existence" of a plot to kill all the Europeans in the country on a specified day. They professed to have documentary evidence of the plot, henceforth known as the "R–Day Plot". It had supposedly been obtained from unnamed informers within the Party. The Royal Commission set up after the Emergency to make findings on the whole state of affairs stated that it could find no evidence whatsoever of the "R–Day" Plot. In subsequent years in discussion with senior Special Branch Officers, when I mentioned this subject they would get quite shifty and be unable to substantiate the plot.

I firmly believe that the so called "Plot" was in fact overkill and was invented by the two Officers, whom I knew well, to ensure a State of Emergency was called. It was unnecessary as there was already enough disturbance to justify calling one.

It is significant to me that the day after Independence was declared in 1964, one of the Officers concerned was immediately deported on the direct orders of Banda and the other, who was on the high seas returning from leave, was turned round in Cape Town and never allowed to set foot in Malawi again! Banda and Co. knew the "R-Day" Plot was a fabrication!

However, back to Mlanje and the closing days of February 1959. The District was in a turmoil and we were working twenty four hours a day. Allan and I were stretched to the limit because there were only the two of us and we did not know which of our seventy odd black Police could be trusted. Many of them we knew through Special Branch were National Party supporters and we did not know how they would react in an Emergency situation. To our relief, at the end of February we welcomed two platoons of white Royal Rhodesian Rifles to support us. A very necessary support. I think in total there were about eighty of them with their Support Staff. They bivvied down in the main Hall of Mlanje Club and all the local wives started the support story with cake baking, barbecues and so on. Allan and I felt a lot safer with these chaps to call on. They were Territorials drawn mainly from the Bulawayo area, all big fresh faced farming lads. Their Platoon Officers I remember were called Jack Dunn and Harry Fox. A splendid set of chaps. Very shortly, a couple of days afterwards, we also received a large contingent of Southern Rhodesian Police, the B.S.A.P., (British South Africa Police), and they were based at Likabula, just round the corner of the mountain. Elsewhere in the country we had contingents of the King's African Rifles, (K.A.R.), the Rhodesian African Rifles, (R.A.R.), the Northern Rhodesian Police and even units from Tanganyika and Uganda. It was, for Nyasaland, a considerable build-up of Force and on 3rd March we learned the reason.

Chapter Seventeen

Operation Sunrise

At midnight on 2nd March, we assembled in the Police Station to be addressed by "Sinbad" Illingworth, the District Commissioner. He was the senior Government Officer and as such was in total charge of the District at a time like this. Present were the B.S.A.P. Commanders and the two RRR Officers, plus a number of others who had hastily been enrolled as Special Constables. These comprised most of the other government officers, the PWD chaps, the Agricultural Officer etc. and managers and assistants from the tea estates. All white of course!

At midnight "Sinbad" opened a sealed envelope which had arrived from Zomba. It was over the signature of the Governor, Sir Robert Armitage, who, having regard to the State of the Country and especially the "R-Day Plot", had declared a 'State of National Emergency'. This conferred enormous powers on the Police and the District Commissioner. "Operation Sunrise" had arrived! Accompanying the Declaration was an Operational Plan which had been worked to a high degree and involved the N.C.P. Party Officials throughout the entire country being arrested at 5am that morning. Each was identified by name together with his title and address. In each case there was an Identifying Officer, usually a Special Branch Sergeant who could physically say, "This is the man", and details of the team ordered to pick him up. The team leaders were mostly white Police Officers or other local senior government officials who had been attested as Specials and the teams were five or six strong, all Specials, plus the Identifying Officer. Throughout the country the teams were to be in position by 4am ready to make an arrest at 5am. The arrested Party Officials were then to be transported to already constructed holding centres in each area for onward transmission out of the country. It was a good plan as far as it went because it was intended to remove all the local and national political heads right out of the country and leave the movement leaderless. This happened, but the speed with which new leaders emerged was amazing!

The Illustrated London News coverage of the arrest of the "gang" leaders

Anyway, in the early hours of 3rd March this was all very exciting and for Allan and me at least, appeared to signal an end to the problems we were having. If only! In my team I had a mixture of young chaps, all from the tea estates, I played rugby and water polo with them and knew I could rely on them.

Allan is a Scotsman and in those days was big and brawny. Amazingly his team comprised wholly Scotsmen from the tea estates. He had not picked them and I could only wonder how such an unholy gang could have got together. Even more amazingly was the fact that Allan's target was – yes – Horace Chikafa. The afore mentioned bete noir!

So, off we went, hearts in our mouths, not knowing if the houses of these people were going to be defended by supporters or what the reaction would be throughout the country when people woke up to find their local leaders spirited away. I cannot remember the name of our pick-up, Bobo something, but there was no trouble at all. We broke down the door of his hut and there he was in bed. The Special Branch Sergeant said this was the man and we grabbed him, put him in our Land Rover and set off for Bvumbwe where our local 'Holding Cage' had been established. As we travelled along the road in the dawn, the other four vehicles of our pick-up parties all fell in line and we travelled in convoy, feeling somewhat safer, to Bvumbwe.

Very exciting on arrival there because there was a large contingent of soldiers, and on one side of the road in the bush, a Saracen Armoured Car with the snout of its gun pointing into the road, and on the other side, a tank with its gun pointing into the road. We dismounted and hauled out of the Land Rover our prisoner, handed him over to the Officer-in-Charge of the Cage, against a signature, and our job was done. Three of the other vehicles did the same but there was no action from Allan Dew's vehicle. I walked over to it and saw that the whole of the tailgate was covered in blood. Allan and his cohorts got out and reached into the back of their vehicle and pulled out what looked like a roll of carpet. It was Horace Chikafa and he looked dead. I asked Allan if he was and he said he didn't know! They handed him over to the Cage Staff who placed him in the middle of the enclosure.

He immediately leaped to his feet shouting "Ufulu", meaning "Freedom". The "Rallying Cry" of National Parties all over Africa. He was bashed about but not seriously injured. Allan said he had attacked them!

Some months later when Lord Devlin conducted the Royal Commission into the Emergency, because Horace Chikafa was a senior Official and there had been violence in this arrest, particular interest was shown.

Allan was subpoenaed to give evidence and he stated that when he and his party had entered Chikafa's house and gone into the bedroom, Chikafa had leaped out of bed and reached under the bed. Thinking he was going for a weapon Allan had seized him and threw him against the wall. The wall at this point had a doorway in it and Chikafa flew out of the doorway cannoning into another Scotsman, Ronnie Greenhill, who was just entering. Greenhill, believing he was being attacked, defended himself and the man was subdued. Lord Devlin said in his Report, and I quote, "The Inspector is a large and powerful man and we found his account most unconvincing!". Allan still maintains this is what happened and obviously I don't know. Lord Devlin didn't believe him though!

Although I was still very young, only twenty-three, I found one aspect of this Emergency quite puzzling, and possibly my thoughts on this could apply in a much larger arena. There is no way that our Emergency could be classed as a "War Situation", it was far too minor and mostly we were not in much danger ourselves.

As I have stated above, most of the Special Constables in our area were drawn from the ranks of the tea planters and their assistants. These were, almost without exception, well brought up young men, I played sport with them and entertained and was entertained by them. If you will remember when I described the tea estates I mentioned that these men controlled vast numbers of black tea pickers. These blacks looked on their "Bwanas" as the fount of their existence. The tea assistant or manager would be the arbiter of their quarrels, their doctor for minor complaints, he ran the Clinic, he organised the Estate School, ran the Estate Shop and the credit accounts of the workers, he decided whether they had a job or not and provided them with housing. I used to think they were like little 'Gods'. And this they all did very willingly, even caringly and fairly. Now suddenly they were Policemen, of a sort. They were able to beat, arrest or even obtain the imprisonment of anybody with the slightest cause. And they did. They became a kind of different being, especially the Scotsmen! The blacks were beaten, kicked, tied up, imprisoned, for the lightest or even no cause. I could not believe how violent they became. I spent a lot of time preventing this treatment and even got a reputation for being a bit soft! And I wasn't. I wondered if this attitude was the seed from which the much larger atrocities perpetrated by very civilised nations, supposedly, on their prisoners in war situations. We were very lucky that there were no repercussions, even after the Devlin Commission which was very searching indeed.

I mentioned above that we were not very confident about the loyalty or commitment of our black Police - and with good cause. Many of them were staunch and utterly loyal to their Officers and the Force, but a large number were either ambivalent or distinctly anti. We had to learn which was which. In the early days of the Emergency I personally went into several riots with a whole platoon of our own Policemen, and having given the order to "Charge", found myself in the middle of the rioting crowd, by myself with a line of sullen looking Policemen just standing back at the edge of the crowd looking on. I managed to extricate myself on each occasion without injury but this could not last forever.

One day we received a report from Bob Bishop, the manager of Thornwood Estate to the effect that there was a large crowd of his workers milling around outside his office threatening to burn it down. "Sinbad" Illingworth sent me off with about a dozen Policemen and a platoon of RRR under the command of Lt. Harry Dunn. The Army in these situations had no powers at all and could not become involved until requested by the senior Police Officer present. This was obviously if he couldn't contain the situation with the forces under his control. The Army thus remained on the back of their three-tonner until asked to assist by me. After receiving a report from Bob Bishop, I de-bussed my Policemen, formed them into a line and read the Official Riot Act to the mob – in Chinyanja. At my side was Harry Dunn. When the crowd failed to disperse, after three warnings I ordered the Police to Charge. They were armed, as I was, with large ash staves specifically designed for use in riots. I also had my service .38 on my belt. Having fought my way some way into this crowd, laying about me with the riot baton, Harry Dunn by my side still, my baton broke off at the handle. Looking round me I realised two things. One, my Policemen had not charged and were standing looking at the crowd, and two, this crowd, unlike previous ones, was quite heavily armed with spears, knobkerries and machetes. They were threatening us and waving their weapons in our faces. Fearing for our lives and also that we might not be able to extricate ourselves, I said to Harry, "We will have to shoot!". Quite a decision for a lad from Maltby Police Station! He agreed and we drew our weapons, in my case a Smith and Wesson .38 and in his case a Browning 9mm automatic. After firing a couple of shots into the air we then fired into the crowd around us. They started to disperse and Harry was able to call his troops off the lorry to hasten their departure. We were shaken but relieved.

There were a number of dead or wounded lying around and for several days afterwards, we were picking up wounded people who reported to the Clinics for treatment. After they were treated they were taken to Court and charged with taking part in a riot. The fact that they were shot was evidence that they were there. Some of the excuses given were ridiculous. One chap said he had been working in his maize garden several miles away when he felt this pain in his leg. Looking down he saw he had been shot! The Magistrate did not believe him!!

Police checking a looted store

The Devlin Commission investigated this

incident which resulted in three deaths and a large number of wounded, and found it to have been completely legal. The riot was established, the Riot Act had been read to them three times in their own language and they failed to disperse. The authorities were then empowered to use all means possible to disperse them.

An interesting sidelight to this incident, subsequently confirmed what had been learned when firearms were used in other incidents and that was the relative uselessness of the .38. A man has to be shot very accurately with a .38 to knock him down. The 9mm will knock him down wherever he is hit. We did not feel very confident of our side-arms after this!

By this time law and order was really out of the window. Hospitals, schools and isolated offices were being destroyed and the militants suddenly realised that the Indian Trading Centres were soft targets. These Indian Trading Centres were scattered all over Central and East Africa in those days and they filled a very real need in the community. They sold clothing, food, fuel, employed a tailor, often had a garage attached to them and were an essential part of the community. Breaking into the stores was easy and emptying them of their goods was easy to accomplish.

Chapter Eighteen

The Limbuli Market Incident

One Saturday night two Indian men came into the Police Station with a complaint. Their store, in fact several stores, at Limbuli, a Trading Centre about thirty miles down the road towards PEA, had been attacked and looting was taking place at that minute. We noticed a lot of blood on the floor round one Indian's foot and asked him where it came from. He pulled a twelve bore shotgun out of his trouser leg and said "Hiding gun down trousers – gun going off – shooting all fingers off foot!". To hide his gun from the looters, he had put it down his trouser leg and it had gone off, taking most of his toes off with it!

"Sinbad" despatched me with about three Land Rovers of Specials to move quickly down to the area and try and catch some of the looters in the act. By this time we had received written authority from the Governor to shoot on sight any person found looting, or anybody found up a telephone pole, (Theft of telephone wire being another of the emerging crimes). There would be no questions, just shoot. "Sindbad" repeated these orders to us before we departed.

It was dark by the time we got there and we approached the Trading Centre round a bend in the road. The centre consisted of half-a-dozen stores spread on either side of the road and as they came into view in our headlights we saw many dozens of Africans come spilling out of the broken windows of each store, carrying bales of cloth, radios, bicycles and everything else comprising the contents of the store. Afterwards we found that the stores were completely emptied. We leaped out of the vehicles and in spite of the Governor's Authority to shoot looters caught in the act, none of us even thought of drawing our weapons. We set off in pursuit of the looters who were disappearing into the bush behind the stores, with and without their booty. I got behind one on a narrow track and chased him. He didn't stop when ordered to and I cracked him on the head with my newly issued riot baton. This had no effect and he kept on running. I kept on whacking him with my baton. Whilst this was going on I heard another chase through a maize field on my left and heard Peter Snell, an erstwhile tea assistant now turned Special Constable cry out, "I'll get you, you bastard", and this was followed by a scream which I thought came from Peter. I continued with my chase, tiring and whacking and eventually the man I was pursuing stopped, bent down and picked up a handful of sand and threw it in my eyes. This terminated the chase and in any case I was shattered by this time. The man then ran on out of sight.

His body was found and taken into one of the local Clinics the following morning. He had struggled home and died from head injuries. I realised I could have achieved the same end, not an objective, legally, by shooting him!

I struggled back to the Trading Centre and found that during his chase Peter Snell had fallen down a ten foot deep brick pit in the middle of a maize field and had broken his arm. That was the end of his Emergency – and rugby for the rest of the season! We had achieved very little with our operation, due largely to the Africans' ability to melt into the bush. However, without doubt they were all local people living within walking distance of Limbuli. We returned to the Boma and reported to "Sindbad" what had happened. Things had reached such a pitch that after consultation with his superior, the Provincial Commissioner, Peter Nicholson, they decided that the following morning a full-scale operation, in strength, would take place in the Limbuli area. Many Forces were moved into the area and these included Nyasaland Police, KAR, RRR, RAR, BSAP, Tanganyikan Police and many Special Constables. The plan was to throw a large ringnet round the entire area and then proceed to search individually, every house inside the net, looking for arms, not a very likely find, and the proceeds of looting. The question was what to do with the people in whose houses looted goods were found. All the Prisons in the country were filled to overflowing, as were the Police Cells and all the temporary "Cages" which had been set up. There was literally nowhere to incarcerate anybody else.

It was then that "Sinbad" had his brainwave. He decided that every house in which loot was found would be burned to the ground. This in itself was illegal and a very serious thing to do to anybody, whether he be an African villager or anybody else anywhere in the world. And the owners of all these houses and any other occupants would be brought to the Market Place in Limbuli where "Sinbad" would decide on their final fate. He issued me and several teams with many boxes of matches, and at dawn we set off. Once the net was in place we set off searching the houses, over a large area. We found many with loot in them and after securing the male occupants, if they were there, a couple of matches under the dry thatched eaves soon had the house going merrily. There were spotter planes overhead and they counted some forty-eight houses burning finally. After about three hours of this we all assembled in the Market Place at Limbuli. There must have been a couple of thousand people there including all the Security Forces and hundreds and hundreds of villagers who had been rounded up, sitting on the ground with their hands on their heads. In the middle of the Market, lying face down, were some forty African males in whose houses loot had been found.

"Sinbad" ordered three forty-four gallon oil drums to be brought to the Market Place and they were laid on their sides, two on the bottom and one on the top. A length of quarter inch square rubber, used by the blacks to fasten goods on the back of their bicycles and sold in the stores was found and it was made into a three ply whip about four feet long. There was total silence whilst the crowd observed these preparations being made.

Then, and I can see this as plainly as yesterday, "Sinbad" addressed the crowd. His Chinyanja was superb, as was that of all the senior Administrative Staff. He stood there, wearing a white shirt and very wide khaki shorts, short socks and thick soled brown shoes. He obtained from the Army an electronic bullhorn and started to speak. He said "Tamverani onse", (Listen to me all of you!). His words were really superb and even if much of what he said was not

AT A BURNT-OUT AFRICAN HOME IN AN AREA WHERE RIOTING BROKE OUT AFTER AN AFRICAN HAD BEEN DETAINED.

Inspector Bean shown in the Illustrated London News

legal, it was very fitting, and as I will explain, did the trick. He told the people that they had been very wicked and that "Queenie", (Queen Elizabeth), was very, very cross with them. He was going to be merciful and not send them to Prison but they were going to be punished. He sentenced them to twenty lashes each from the whip. Now as the senior Magistrate in the District he was entitled to impose sentences of Corporal Punishment which was still legal then but no one could ever have called what had taken place "Legal Proceedings!" However, what else could be done with them under the circumstances? And it was a punishment they understood! He then said that one each from the Nyasaland Police, the BSAP, the Army and the Special Constables would carry out the punishment. Ten culprits each. I was selected to be the Nyasaland Police Officer to start the proceedings. One man was selected and tied face down on the pile of drums. I then took up my place and started. "Sinbad" counted the number of strikes, in Chinyanja over the bullhorn. I'm afraid that I was very apprehensive of appearing brutal or to be enjoying the action and did not lay too heavily into the man. There were soon mutters, especially from the Specials, to the effect that I was not going hard enough and was too soft! I was glad when my share was over. I must say that although the rubber certainly hurt the culprits, it only raised red weals and did not cut them as a real Judicial Flogging often did.

Eventually the proceedings were done with and after further admonitions from "Sinbad", they were dismissed and told not to do it again. The effectiveness of this operation could be seen in that there were no more major incidents in our area and furthermore, when the Devlin Commission held its hearings, although there were many complaints about the burning of houses, not a single word was heard about the floggings. They knew punishment was earned and considered it to be fair – under the circumstances. The Devlin Commission did find the burning of villagers' houses to be illegal and reprehensible though.

On returning to the Boma "Sinbad" declared the whole area to be "Officially Closed", he could do this, and set up roadblocks to stop the Press from entering. The International Press by this time was in great evidence in the country. One roadblock was on the main road south of the Boma just outside the town. The Sergeant manning the block came into the Police Station shortly after setting it up and said that three journalists with cameras had told him they had permission from the Provincial Commissioner to enter the area and photograph it and he let them through – then thought to check if everything was in order. "Sinbad" was furious and sent me off in pursuit with orders to arrest the three. I found them about twenty miles down the road, considering where they would start taking pictures. To their very great and vociferous protestations I did arrest them and took them back to "Sinbad". He 'read them the riot act' and kicked them out of the area with instructions not to return.

They did however return, the next day, with a written authority from the Provincial Commissioner to enter the area! "Sinbad" could do little now except let them in and send me along to escort them, (to ensure their safety!!), and to make sure they didn't see anything they shouldn't. Off we went and soon became quite amicable. I did draw the line against running over a catwalk over a raging river with my revolver in my hand, to simulate the chase of a rioter! I allowed myself to be photographed standing in the smoking ruins of a house with my hands on my hips, and my .38 in its holster! The following week the photo appeared in the London Illustrated News over the caption, "A Police Officer investigates the burning of a house by dissidents in the Mlanje area". As I had burned it myself the day before it didn't need much investigation!

As I have said, after this operation, things started to get back to normal in Mlanje and the rest of the country settled down. The Devlin Commission came and went and submitted its report in due course. The Emergency had cost some three million pounds, a lot of money in those days, one white person lost his life and I think about twenty-eight black people. The African National Congress, having been banned by the Government, simply renamed itself the Malawi Congress Party, which it is to this day and as the Party Officials, taken outside the country after Operation Sunrise, returned, they resumed their positions, albeit under the new name. Eventually as everybody knows, they became the ruling party on Independence being granted and the whole of the Emergency proved to have been a waste of time, and at most a delaying tactic by the British Government.

I cannot leave Mlanje without a few words about our Medical Officers. They were in the main a splendid group of people, working with limited resources and often, as was the case at Mlanje, without electricity. They found their work greatly interesting, having to deal with so many ailments and injuries of types they would never have encountered in the UK. I remember one M.O. telling me in the Club about an African who had been admitted that day with a six-inch nail driven so tightly into his skull that it was impossible to get even a fingernail under the head. The nail was removed under anaesthetic and there appeared to be no damage done! The Patient left Hospital a couple of days later and resumed his normal life!

One "Ailment" they could never get to grips with was that of a Witchdoctor's Curse. If an African was cursed and told to die by a witchdoctor, he did just that. Their faces would turn grey and they would stop eating. Their relatives brought them to the Hospital but nothing our Doctors could do would convince them they were not going to die, and in a few days or weeks, they did. The only possible cure was to find an even more powerful witchdoctor to remove the curse and this was rarely possible.

One of our Doctors, (there was only one stationed in Mlanje but they only stayed a year or so and moved on), was a delightful Irishman named Charles Treston. I played Snooker with Charles, who was a very good player, and socialised with him. His treatments were legend however. Feeling out-of-sorts or with a definite illness you would go to him and describe your problem. He would scratch his head and say, "That's interesting. What do you think it is?". When you said you didn't know and that was why you had come to him, he would open his desk drawers, rummage around and produce a bottle of pills saying, "Take these for a couple of days and see what they do. If they don't work come back and we'll try something else!" Very reassuring I must say!

Then one day I went to him with a problem with my eyes. He put some drops in the eyes and took me into the storeroom where it was pitch black and used an instrument to look into my eyes. He explained that the drops were Atropine which dilated the pupil so he could look inside the eye. Having found nothing wrong we went outside and of course, I was totally blinded by the bright sunlight because my pupils were wide open. He told me to go away and wait to see if the problem disappeared. I asked him if he was going to administer an antidote so that my eyes would return to normal and he said he was sorry but they had run out of the antidote! I would have to wait for it to wear off naturally. He had to drive me home because I couldn't see and it took two days to clear. The only advantage was that I could see perfectly in the dark!

Most of them accepted that a part of the job was the endless post mortem examinations which had to be carried out. Some of them were very good and I learned a lot from them and others I felt I could do a better job myself. I felt sorry for one chap named Murray who, when he had not been there for very long, threw his instruments down in mid-examination and walked out of the mortuary saying, "I'm doing no more of this. What you need is a bloodsucking cannibal!". I resisted the temptation to tell him that one of his predecessors came pretty close to this description! It needed a telephone call from the District Commissioner to the Provincial Medical Officer to get him to continue the PM and he was shortly afterwards transferred to a District without such a high death rate.

One day I was called into the Officer-in-Charge's office and told that I was to be transferred to a command of my own at Kasungu in the Central Province. A couple of weeks later I set off on the drive North followed by a three ton truck with my belongings piled on the back with Zebio sitting on the top of the whole lot.

Chapter Nineteen

Kasungu

Although Kasungu was a much larger District in size than Mlanje, it didn't have anything like the same size population. Large areas formed part of the Kasungu Game Reserve, which was unfenced and there were quite a lot of large rivers. The whole length of the western side of the District was contiguous with Northern Rhodesia. There was a great deal of game of all kinds including the "Big Five", that is Elephant, Rhino, Lion, Leopard and Buffalo both within and without the Game Reserve. Having a smaller population to service, the Boma staff was

Kasungu
(From Wikipedia)
Kasungu is a Town in the Central Region of Malawi. It is approximately 130 kilometres (81 mi) North-West of the Capital of Malawi, Lilongwe, and is 35 kilometres (22 mi) East of Kasungu National Park. The main Industry in Kasungu is Tobacco-Growing.

A farm close to Kasungu was the Birthplace of the first President of Malawi, Dr. Hastings "Kamuzu" Banda and it is a "stronghold" of the Malawi Congress Party.

correspondingly smaller than that in Mlanje. There were only seven families, with no children resident, in the Boma and the rest of the white population in the District could not have numbered more than a couple of hundred, if that, being tobacco farmers, groundnut farmers and quasi-Government Marketing Board officials.

Topographically it was not too interesting being composed mainly of Mopani bush and Dambos, (Vleis or water meadows), a kind of Savannah type country. Immediately south of the Boma, about two miles away, a large Koppie, (a conical pointed hill), dominated the landscape. This was known, fairly kindly as "Kasungu Mountain" and was in fact one thousand feet above the surrounding land. A pinprick after what I was accustomed to in Mlanje!

Kasungu's main claim to fame was that it was the birthplace of Dr. Hastings "Kamuzu" Banda and as a result he came there quite often. We were always notified of his intended visits and I met him on a number of occasions. There was no apparent sign of his megalomania at that time, what megalomania there was was shown on his behalf by his lieutenants, Aleke Banda, Chipembere and Co, all of whom he eventually had killed! He later had a massive Palace constructed on the slopes of "Kusungu Mountain" but this was after my time.

Another sidelight on Dr. Banda was shown when he ordered the very best Mercedes Benz 600 through the local Agents, 'R.W. Gunston Ltd'. I was fortunate enough to be in Gunstons when the car arrived, accompanied by a top Mechanic from the Factory in Germany. It was the custom of both Mercedes and Rolls Royce at that time when an ordered car such as the top "Merc" or a "Roller" arrived at its destination, for a telegram to be sent to the Factory whereupon a Mechanic would be despatched forthwith to unpack the car from its packing case, put it on the road and teach whoever was to take care of the car and how to look after it. The Mechanic showed me round the car and it was truly a magnificent vehicle with every possible feature fitted. But when Gunstons submitted the bill for payment however, it was ignored. After repeated requests eventually Banda's office replied that they were not responsible for the payment as Banda considered the car a gift from "the grateful people of the German Democratic Republic!". They had to write it off and I do not know who eventually met the cost, either Mercedes, Gunstons or the German Government!

Whilst on the subject of luxury cars I must recount the tale of the Provincial Education Officer in Dedza in the Central Province. He drove an incredible car considering the roads and the terrain he had to traverse. It was a black 1928 Rolls Royce. He could not get the proper tyres for it in Nyasaland and so ran it on a set of tractor front wheel tyres, the kind with longitudinal ribs round them. At one stage he decided that his gearbox was whining and wanted to fix it himself. He did maintain the car himself and so wrote to Rolls Royce in England, explaining that he had a 1928 Roller, chassis and engine number supplied, with then 250 000 miles on the clock and he felt that the gearbox was whining. Both the gearbox and the differential were sealed units and he could not get into them. Would Rolls Royce please give him instructions as to how to get into the gearbox and what to do.

Their response was brief, to the point and arrogant and he had it framed on the wall of his office afterwards. It said words to the effect,

"Dear Sir,

If you own a 1928 Rolls Royce with only 250 000 miles on the clock, the gearbox and the differential are not whining!

Yours faithfully etc."

What confidence!

Anyway, apart from taking up our time, Dr. Banda's visits to Kasungu were not a problem at that time as he was virtually, then, a 'non-person'.

Chapter Twenty

Game and Poaching in Kasungu

Crime in the District was much less spectacular and violent than Mlanje and comprised the usual offences against property, lesser crimes against the person and far fewer murders. The major difference was the incidence of deaths by wild animals. Herds of elephants roamed the area and at the right time of the year would raid the villagers' maize fields, destroying an entire village's staple food for one year in one evening. In attempting to drive them off it was not unusual for a man to get too close to an elephant and it would turn and kill him, trampling him into the ground, sometimes after tearing him in half! We used to have to go out and literally pick up the pieces if the hyenas had not got there first. Along the banks of the bigger rivers villagers would get in the way of hippo returning to the water after a night's foraging and it is well known how dangerous it is to get between a hippo and water. One snap in passing and the villager would be halved! It is said that hippo are responsible for killing more people than any other animal in Africa. Around the rivers also crocodiles took their usual percentage of life. Marauding lion and leopard were occasionally responsible for killings and we still had the hyena problem, albeit not on the Mlanje scale.

Poaching was also a big problem and as I was, ex-Officio, also the local Game Control Officer this took up quite a lot of our time, although I enjoyed immensely being out amongst the game. The Africans, quite understandably, could not see why they could not kill wild animals for food. The game belonged to no one, it was roaming on free land, they had always lived on it, there being virtually no beef in the area, only a few sheep, and they thought it was there for the taking. They could in fact buy a Resident's Game Licence for five Pounds as I did and with this could shoot an enormous variety and amount of meat but they didn't see why they should. Five Pounds represented a large percentage of the rural African's income! When we caught them, we had to take them to Court and I always felt sorry for them.

One case in particular remains in my mind though and this was a party which was hunting elephant, for meat. I will digress for a moment and say that it never ceased to amaze me that we could walk for many hours hunting game, (legally!!), and be many miles from the nearest village and as soon as we shot something, within an hour or so there would be many Africans appearing from the bush, "To help you cut up and carry the meat back Bwana!". How they knew we had shot something I never learned. Bush telegraph!

So, this group of Africans were hunting elephant for meat, and an elephant would provide food for a large village for a long time. They rarely had proper firearms and often used snares, even for elephant, a very cruel method of hunting, but they did obtain rudimentary and home-made guns. These were made of a simple length of piping, a roughly hewn stock and some primitive firing mechanism using black powder which was easily available. They would pack the barrel, (a tube), with wadding of some kind, pour in any kind of chunks of metal they could find, nuts and bolts or whatever, pack it again with wadding and set off to look for some prey. The guns had no range and very little hitting power and were obviously extremely dangerous, and illegal! The party in question found their elephant and crept closer to it. The designated "Gunman" had to creep right up to the elephant's side without it seeing him, place the gun against its side and fire it. In this instance, the gun exploded, succeeding in killing the elephant which promptly fell on the gunman killing him too!!

When we got there, we first had to organise the cutting up of the elephant before we could recover the squashed body of the gunman. Not much problem with a PM there either!

My new District Commissioner at Kasungu was as far removed a man from "Sinbad" Illingworth as could be imagined. "Sinbad" was macho, fair, determined, Cricket mad and a man to be respected. Michael was of undetermined sexual orientation, slightly built, quite uninterested in sport and more suited to running a knitting circle. I had heard that he was a nightmare during The Emergency which fortunately was all but finished by the time I got to Kasungu. He had married, to everyone's amazement, a very nice woman who was the District Medical Officer and who frequently told her friends that she, "Had great difficulty getting him to perform!". Whatever that meant! My main reason for mentioning him is that he owned a very beautiful Siamese cat to which I will return.

I found that the Boma at Kasungu was plagued with hyenas which scavenged around the houses at night. Nothing vaguely edible was left outside the houses by the owners or it would be eaten. Cured skins left over the back of verandah furniture lasted very briefly and dustbins had to be securely fastened down. I volunteered to try and eradicate the nuisance. It was believed that some of them hung out in the Donga nearby, (a dried up river bed), behind the D.C.'s house, and came out to forage at night.

One night when darkness was fully established I ventured into the donga carrying a twelve bore shotgun and wearing a night-light. This was a hunting lamp attached to the forehead, not unlike a Miner's lamp. It picked up dozens of pairs of eyes, night apes, genet cats, buck and others between which I was not at that time able to differentiate. Eventually I spotted a pair of eyes which I felt were big enough, and bright enough, to be those of a hyena. I let go with the shotgun and the eyes disappeared at once. Sure I had it I went closer and found to my dismay that there, stone dead, was the D.C.'s Siamese cat! I fled the area and when I began to hear stories of the disappearance of the cat, was one of the most concerned! I never told anybody about this of course but I would have been finished with the D.C. had this become known.

The hyenas continued to raid chicken houses and were an absolute nuisance. During this time I became an avid hunter, there being so much game in Kasungu and the whole time I lived there, I lived on game meat, there being little more than sheep or chickens to eat otherwise. Although hunting is much frowned on these days one has to remember that this was over fifty years ago and there was very abundant game in much of Central and East Africa. Hunting, with a licence, was legal and a way of life and I hunted three or four times a week, always for meat. I only once shot anything that couldn't be eaten, otherwise it was for food or protection of people or livestock.

Although in the Kasungu area there was virtually every kind of game animal to be found, some were more rare than others. Sable antelope, (now fully protected and quite rare), as are Roan antelope, were very common and I shot quite a few. Eland, the biggest of all antelope, often larger than cows, were not so common and ran in herds varying in size from twenty or thirty to over a hundred. They made superb eating. I was there for sometime before I got my first eland and when I did, its horns and skullcap were mounted on a wooden plaque to adorn the walls of my khonde alongside previous kills. Not "PC" today I know but the norm in those days. Not long after I proudly mounted the horns on my khonde walls, I was having my breakfast one day when I noticed that the horns were no longer there. Instead were two large muddy paw marks. The mfisi, (hyena), had pinched them. I was furious!! The fact that they were so green and hadn't cured had attracted the mfisi. I decided to set up a trap gun on my khonde and bait it with a sheep's head. This consisted simply of lashing a loaded, cocked shotgun to a framework I erected outside my front door and securing the sheep's head to the muzzle of the shotgun. From the sheep's head ran a cord, around the back of the trigger guard and then tied to both triggers of the shotgun. The theory being that when the mfisi pulled the head off the muzzle of the gun, it would pull the string thus discharging both barrels into the mfisi's head and killing it. This kind of thing usually worked although it was my first attempt at doing it!!

However, that night I had just gone to bed and sleep when I was awoken by a loud knocking on my front door. Thinking this was hardly likely to be the hyena knocking I screamed, "Don't move an inch", and ran down my passage to the front door. Standing there was another Police Officer, one David Searle, travelling to the North and looking for shelter for the night. I lighted a lantern, all the while adjuring him not to move and carefully let him in. Once in I disarmed the shotgun and showed him what a narrow escape he had had. I must say we were both somewhat pale by the thought of what might have happened. Never before, or again, did somebody come to my door in the night – but what a tragedy it could have been!

It can be seen that the mfisi were winning this battle and I was determined they wouldn't so I developed another ploy. I went to the market and purchased a whole ox head. In the evening I tied it with a rope to the tailgate of the Police Land Rover and dragged it all around the Boma making trails which always lead back to my front garden. With some huge stakes I fastened the head down on my front lawn and about ten at night, once the Boma had bedded down, wrapped myself in a blanket on the roof of the khonde, armed with a large headlamp and my shotgun. I was sure that the mfisi would come and I was close enough to let them have a full blast from the shotgun. Well, I sat there from about ten at night until four the next morning and not a thing moved. Tired and disappointed I climbed down and went to bed for a couple of hours. I was up just after six and lo-and-behold, score yet again to the mfisi. The head was totally gone, not a shred of bone or meat left!! I had done my best, it was not good enough and the mfisi won the final battle. I gave up after this!

Hunting was my major occupation at Kasungu, whatever the season and I walked many, many miles. I would get up at about four o'clock, drive to a known hunting area, pick-up one or two hunting boys who knew the area and walk out from the village. Sometimes we would walk a whole day, perhaps ten or twelve hours without seeing anything, maybe twenty or thirty miles, others, we would walk perhaps only an hour and shoot something. This we would butcher, carry back to the village and the Land Rover the meat I wanted, i.e. the hind quarters and the fillets, putting the rest up a tree away from the mfisi and under cover so the vultures could not see it. The villagers would then return to collect the balance of the meat, really the major portion, for their own use. My Policemen used to get a good share and my friends and I also shared the rest. I once shot three kudu one morning and I counted that eighty-four people ate from them.

One of my favourite areas was a village called Linyangwa and this was the closest village to the Reserve. The boundary of the Reserve was a dambo stretching several miles called Lisitu. The game of course didn't know it represented the edge of the area where they were safe so it was a good hunting area. The Africans used to burn off the grass in the dry season and about ten days after the burning, green shoots used to come through and this attracted the game. On Christmas Eve 1959 I promised my Policemen that I would shoot a couple of buck for their Christmas Dinner and off I went to Linyangwa. My hunting boys there were Richard Shaba and Siki Banda, both employed as Game Guards by the Game Dept. and as they patrolled every day, they knew where we were most likely to find game. In the middle of the afternoon we were following fresh tracks of a herd of hartebeest when we walked into a dense thicket. In the middle of it I thought war had suddenly broken out! There was a huge explosion of sound and disturbance of the bush and my main impression was of this huge black backside disappearing out of the far side of the thicket. We had walked right on top of a resting black rhino and were very lucky it left in the direction it did, not our direction! No meat for the Polisi that Christmas! We retired discreetly.

The Game Guards were very confident with wild animals, being in contact with them every day and were armed with only .303 rifles, really quite useless for game. I was walking one morning with Richard Shaba on Lisitu again when as we came round a corner we saw seven lion about twenty yards from us! It was my first encounter with lion and I was riveted to the spot. Not so Richard Shaba. He instantly pulled off his hat and waving it ran straight at the lion shouting, "Ndili Muntu", literally, "I am a man". The lion straight away all turned tail and ran away as fast as they could. I was filled with admiration but never tried that stunt myself.

The lion of course weren't hungry, are very idle and perceived Richard as a threat. The best bet for them was to run!

Lion were not that common in Kasungu although I saw quite a few over my time there but I used to see them often on the back of a Land Rover when I went to Lilongwe, our Provincial Capital, for shopping. Lilongwe was about seventy miles from Fort Manning on the Northern Rhodesia Border. On the other side of the Border was Fort Jameson. Fort Jameson was on the edge of what was, and still is, one of the best Game Reserves in Africa, the Luangwa Valley. The residents of the Fort Jameson area also used to come to Lilongwe to do their shopping and amongst them was a chap called Norman Carr, a Game Ranger in Luangwa. He had picked up two abandoned male lion cubs when they were very young and adopted them and brought them up. They went everywhere with him but when he came to Lilongwe they had to be confined. He had a kind of cage built onto the back of his Land Rover and used to leave these two lions, named 'Big Boy' and 'Little Boy', who were very big by the time I saw them, in the back of the Land Rover whilst he did his shopping. Nobody of course went near his vehicle and the lion just lazed and slept in the back. He probably did the same job as George Adamson in Kenya but didn't enjoy, and probably didn't want, the same publicity.

Kasungu had a joint border with Northern Rhodesia and I was told that just over the border at a place called Lundazi, level with Kasungu, was a full-scale castle on a Lake where it was possible to get a very good meal and to fish in the lake. I got a local African to guide me along small tracks and eventually emerged on a road which lead to this castle. What an incongruous sight it was, stuck there in the middle of the bush. In fact, it was just a Government Rest House built by the local D.C. who happened to have a flair for the exotic. It was very authentic and beautiful and set on the side of a large dam full of bream and as one fished, game was constantly coming down to drink on the far side of the dam. I took the opportunity to visit the Lundazi Boma and introduce myself to a very surprised white Police Inspector who was my opposite number there, albeit a hundred miles or so away.

Lundazi Castle

Chapter Twenty-One

Help at Last – of a Kind!

An interesting event for the Nyasaland Police occurred whilst I was at Kasungu. Following discussion between the Government of Nyasaland and the British Government it was realised, as a result of the Emergency, that the practice of having only one white Police Officer on most Stations with the black Police not being 100% reliable was not good for security. The situation was changed immediately in the short term by drafting in a number of white Assistant Inspectors from the Northern Rhodesian Police. One was sent to me in Kasungu. I have to confess that he was not much use at all and in conference with my colleagues we found we all felt the same. The feeling was that the NRP had sent along the chaps they could most easily do without because they were no good. There was not much support from them and the one I had with me managed to lose my dog on "Kusungu Mountain" in the end!

However this situation changed dramatically when we received a large contingent, about seventy I think, of British Police Officers on secondment for a year. They were mainly Sergeants from Forces all over Britain with a few Inspectors thrown in for weight. The Sergeants became temporary Inspectors and the Inspectors became temporary Superintendents. They were a great bunch of chaps and although their experience of Africa was totally nil, their Police experience was invaluable. I received a Metropolitan Police Sergeant named Dennis Watson. He was a very huge man and strangely for those days, was a white Mohammedan. There was a Mosque in Kasungu and he asked me for permission each Friday to change into civilian clothes and attend the midday Service. He looked so strange, trotting off down the main, (the only), road to the Mosque wearing his little round white hat. Our black Police and the locals were intensely intrigued by the whole situation!

Dennis was a lovely man though and he stayed with me in my house and we had a lot of fun together. He was also an avid bird watcher, accustomed to the Essex marshes. The bird life in Nyasaland was, and is, stupendous and he thought he was in heaven. He had thought to provide himself with Roberts Book on "Birds of Southern Africa", the "Bible" in Africa for bird watchers and so was well prepared for identification.

This was especially useful for me because I used to do a lot of duck shooting at Kasungu. We had two large rivers, the Buwa and the Rusa which merged on a huge wetland, about thirty miles from the Boma and we used to go down before dawn, get ourselves hidden in the reeds on the edge of the river and wait for dawn to come. Prolific is an inadequate word to describe the wealth of bird life there and Dennis was in paradise. With his large binoculars he was able to say, a bunch of this or that coming down river about two hundred yards away and I could be prepared. Although I offered him a gun he would not shoot. We could easily bring back up to a hundred birds for a morning's shooting and the cook boy and his friends had a busy time plucking, gutting and preparing the birds for the deep freeze. We soon got through them because if we had people for dinner and cooked duck for them, we always cooked twice as many as we needed because one never knew how many "rubber" ducks one had. When you are shooting at a flight of duck, you can't tell which are the young ones and which ones the old tough 'uns. Likewise you don't have time to pick out the pretty ones! The excess birds never went to waste, as they were good to eat cold and of course the cook boy got his share! One problem with shooting duck there was that the rivers were full of crocodiles and if you knocked a bird down in the water, it stayed there. But only for a short while then with a rush it would disappear under the water grabbed by some foraging croc! We could not use dogs of course because the crocs would have got them too!! We tried therefore to knock them down over the land. The shooting as a whole in Kasungu was great but the duck shooting would make almost any English duck shooter totally green with envy.

One experience I had at Kasungu, whilst I am sure was not unique for

A group of UK Police Officers seconded to the British Police Unit in Nyasaland during the Rhodesian/Nyasaland Emergency, Aug 1960 to Feb 1961

a Police Officer, was certainly unusual. Normally we come on the scene of suicides or attempted suicides after the event but in this case I actually witnessed the attempt. We had in Nyasaland a number of Farmers' Marketing Boards which purchased produce from farmers, often at a controlled price, and sold the produce on. In Kasungu the Farmers Marketing Board, (FMB) handled tobacco and groundnuts grown by the local Africans. Elsewhere it might be cotton or coffee. There are two main types of tobacco produced, Flue Cured where the picked tobacco leaves are cured in huge tall barns in a controlled temperature and humidity, and then there is Sun-Dried, used by the Africans where the tobacco leaves are simply laid out on racks in the sun and left to dry naturally. The latter is purchased by the FMB whilst the former was sold directly on the Auction Floors in Limbe. When the tobacco and groundnut seasons come round, the local offices of the FMB carried very large amounts of money. Often on an open three ton truck they would transport from Lilongwe to Kasungu several hundred thousand pounds in cash so the FMB could buy the produce. It was a lot of money then and is even now. I often marvelled that nobody ever thought to knock it off! The border was not far away and with the poor communications then existing, a thief could very easily be out of the country before the theft was discovered. I never heard of it happening though but I would give it a life span of five minutes on the road now! The local manager was a great friend of mine called George Perry and he was assisted by a nice little chap called Cecil Stone. One day George came to my office and told me he had discovered during the course of a random audit that several thousand pounds had been embezzled from their funds by very primitive means, and it was obvious that Cecil Stone had done it. He had tackled him and Cecil had admitted the theft and had retired to his house and was drinking.

George and I then drove down to Cecil's house where we found him knocking back brandies and coke steadily. I discussed the situation with him and he was very morose. He kept getting up and refurbishing his drink and after one such visit to his bar, sat down and said something to the effect that he was done for now and would end his life. Saying which he took another swig of his drink, emptying the glass. I said, "Don't be silly Cecil, we'll sort something out" and he said "Too late, I've done it". I asked him what he had done and he said the glass he had just drunk contained poison. He wouldn't tell us what it was so we looked around and found an empty tube of rat poison containing phosphorous. We asked him if this was what he had taken and he said he had put the whole tube in his last drink. I dashed back to the local Hospital and found that the Doctor, the District Commissioner's wife, was away shopping in Lilongwe. The black Medical Aid at the Hospital told us that the best we could do was to stomach pump poor Cecil. He wouldn't attempt the job himself but gave us the equipment and a large quantity of permanganate of potash, purple in colour, which he said was an antidote for phosphorous. I took this back to Cecil's house by which time he had lost consciousness, although I believe this was more due to the alcohol rather than the poison. Anyway, George and I had to force this tube down his throat until we thought we had reached his stomach and then pump gallons, or so it seemed, of this purple liquid down him. It immediately all came back up, presumably with the phosphorous and he regained a very shaky consciousness. A couple of hours later we took him through to the bigger Hospital in Lilongwe from where he was discharged the next day. FMB did not prosecute him and he paid back the money which was missing and that was an end to the matter. I found it rather bizarre at the time though, to have witnessed him actually trying to take his own life!

Chapter Twenty-Two

Anjoka – Snakes!

As I read through what I have written I become aware that I have not written very much about snakes, a creature one associates strongly with Africa. The main reason for this is that they never presented much of a problem. I remember in my early days at Mlanje the cook boy calling me one day to come and look at this snake crossing the track outside my house. I was staggered to see an enormous body entirely filling the track which

African Python

was about fourteen feet wide. I could see neither the head nor the tail of what had to be a large python. Pythons are relatively harmless to man and are not poisonous although their bite can turn very nasty owing to their dirty teeth. A python the size of the one I was looking at could easily swallow a man whole after first constricting him. They would not normally attack a man either but it has been known. I saw a smaller python which had swallowed a large goat and it was a sight to behold. The animal is swallowed whole after the python has disengaged its lower jaw to accommodate the size. If possible they then make for the nearest water in which they lie for a couple or more days until the animal is totally digested.

Whilst I was in Kasungu, one late afternoon my cook boy came running in and said, "You must come quickly with your shottigun. There is a snake at the Bwana Doctor's house". Allan Pugh the District Surgeon lived next door to me so, grabbing my shotgun I ran next door where an agitated Allan took me into his lounge and pointed to a thin grey snake about four feet long which was curled up on his Radio. I thought it was a Skaapsteker, a not very poisonous snake.

He said excitedly to me, "Shoot it. Shoot it!". I was amazed and pointed out that if I shot the snake I would also blow his Radio to kingdom come! He hadn't thought about that side of it. So we disposed of the snake by picking it up, balanced on the end of a fencing foil, and depositing it in the garden where it made good its escape.

A popular myth, often quoted by Africans, is that there is never one snake without another, its mate nearby. They insist on killing all "njokas" as they call them and then burning the body, thus preventing the mate from joining it. There is no foundation for this belief but I must tell a short story illustrating why they might think so. Or perhaps I am stupid! I was out hunting in the Tuli Block, on the border between Southern Rhodesia and Bechuanaland,

Puff Adder

once with my friend John Ilsley when we found a small puff adder in the path, about eighteen inches long. These are very poisonous snakes whose bite mortifies flesh where they bite. They are not likely to kill a man unless he perhaps has a heart condition or something and cannot stand the shock. When John and I found this small puff adder, we killed it by simply standing on its head and crushing it. This was in the days before I stopped killing snakes. I have many times been criticised since for rescuing snakes and putting them to safety rather than kill them. Many people just say, "Kill all snakes". They are beautiful creatures and intend no harm to man. I am not one of these "nutters" who play with snakes and inevitably end up, even after many years, by being bitten, I just think they should live. Anyway, after killing this puff adder John and I continued on our hunt and several hours later as we passed the spot where we had killed the snake, we were amazed to find another puff adder, of identical size lying exactly on top of, and exactly along the contours of the snake we had killed! I cannot explain this but perhaps the Africans are right after all?

I mention "nutters" with regard to snakes and to illustrate, I once, while on holiday, visited the Snake Park in Bulawayo. It was deserted and the Curator offered to take us round personally which I thought was very pleasant of him. He showed us this and that and then we came to a glass cage with a large puff adder in it. In the corner of the cage was a jam jar filled with fluid with a strange object in the fluid. I asked him what it was and he said it was his forefinger!! I then noticed that his right hand was bandaged. Apparently a couple of weeks before he was putting on a display for visitors, with bare hands, utterly foolish and a clear case of familiarity breeding contempt. The snake had turned and had bitten him on the forefinger. He immediately drove himself to the Bulawayo General Hospital where they pumped the area full of antivenine, (Anti-venom) – to no avail. The flesh surrounding the bite died and they had to amputate the finger at the base. So he put it on display with the snake that had done it! No accounting for tastes.

It is a general belief that all animals are born with a natural instinct for survival but I wonder if this is always the case. I once visited the Snake Park at Kariba in Rhodesia at a time when they were feeding the snakes with their once weekly meal. In a cage with a very large cobra, about eight feet long, they had placed about a dozen day-old chicks, still alive. The cobra will only eat live food. The chicks wandered about the cage, quite without fear until the snake fixed one of them with its gaze, slithered forward and bit it. They do not inject venom unless it is necessary and with something as small as a chick, simply biting it and holding on will kill it. When the chick was dead, the snake unhinged its jaw and slowly worked the chick down its throat, head first so the wings and legs would not catch on the way down. This all took some time and whilst it was going on, the other chicks wandered around quite unconcerned and indeed one of them climbed up on top of the cobra's head and stood looking down its throat watching its mate disappear! I could not believe this because I thought the chicks, and all animals, would have an inborn fear of anything dangerous, especially snakes. Perhaps they are taught danger by their mothers? Anyway, the rest of the chicks all went the same way over the next hour or so. The curator told me that a few nights before, one of the large cobras had escaped and got into the store where they kept the live feed for the snakes. It had got into a box of two dozen chicks and ate the lot. When they came in in the morning it was lying there, comatose and stuffed!

I enjoyed a great eighteen months in Kasungu but before I left to go on my first Overseas Leave, one further adventure was to present itself. In 1960 the Queen Mother paid an Official Visit to the Federation and part of that included a visit to Nyasaland, in particular the Lakeshore. The nearest place on the Lake to Kasungu was a place called Salima where there were three Lakeside Hotels. The one in the middle was called "Grand Beach" and to give the Queen Mum respite from her Official Duties it was arranged that she should have an hour and a half's seclusion right on the beach by the lakeside. They erected a nice little lapa, (a palm covered shelter), for her to sit in and the view was marvellous for her – and a lovely rest. Some brain however thought the view could be improved by having a water skier pulled past her shelter as she sat. Enquiries revealed that I could ski and I was deputed for the job! As soon as she had entered the hotel, I abandoned my post where I was controlling security and shot off to the hotel in the next bay. A quick change, out onto the lake behind a boat and then I was pulled away and across the Queen Mum's view. As I passed her, about fifty yards out, she waved to me and I waved back. Round the next headland, turn round and repeat the, performance back across her bay. We waved again and then I was out of sight back where I started. Into the hotel, a quick change back into uniform and away to my security point. I would imagine as she passed me in her car on the way out and I saluted her past, she had no idea she had already seen me. A lovely memory for me though to take on leave.

The Queen Mother when she visited Nyasaland

Chapter Twenty-Three

UK Leave

Off I went on "Home Leave" to the UK handing over Kasungu to my colleague John ("Tennis") Parker, so called to distinguish him from my other colleague, John ("Alcohol") Parker. Both names being totally descriptive. J.T. Parker was also a hunter but he enjoyed a rather more hazardous experience than I had done. He also went to Linyangwa to hunt but instead of taking at least one hunting boy with him, he went by himself. There was a heavy heat haze and he couldn't see the sun and there were no mountains or koppies with which he could orientate himself. He became lost and had to climb a tree for the night to avoid a pack of hyenas which found him. He had no water and there was none in the bush. He walked all day, afterwards clearly in the wrong direction and the same day the villagers noticed his Land Rover parked outside their village. They reported this to the Boma and it was obvious J.T. Parker was missing whilst hunting in the bush. The alarm was raised and the PMF was brought up from Zomba to conduct a search. On the third day 200 of them spread out in a line several miles wide and set off down Lisitu looking for signs of John T. Parker. At four in the afternoon of that, the third day, the last man in the line spotted John in the distance staggering in the general direction of Northern Rhodesia. He said that if he had got nowhere that night, he would have shot himself. The previous night he had been treed by a pack of hyenas again. He was saved but there is a nice post script to this story as John le Mesurier, the Assistant Commissioner in charge of Central Province, wrote him a letter telling him how pleased he was that he had been saved and advising him that he would be docked three days leave for the time he had been missing!

So off I went to Paris where I picked up a brand-new Peugeot car which I drove around France for a while and then back to my home town of Doncaster. I had achieved my Father's dream and here I was, a young Colonial Police Officer, with a lovely new car in England.

It was expected that during the six-months' leave we enjoyed every three years that we would take a course of some kind germane to our work. It might be Fingerprints and Photography, a Senior C.I.D. Course, a Special Branch Course, or for senior Officers, the Senior Officers' Course at Ryton. I opted for the Senior C.I.D. Course held at Bishopsgarth in Wakefield, at the Headquarters of my old Force, the West Riding. The other option open to me was the same course at Hendon near London. Naturally I wanted to stay in Yorkshire near my family.

So early in November 1960 I presented myself at Bishopsgarth Detective

Training School for the three months course which was to follow. We had been booked into "digs" for the duration and I was pleased to find that I was to share with two chaps from Northern Rhodesia, Paul Fillery and Mike Davis and a D/Sgt. from Nottinghamshire, Archie Dove. Our Course Instructor was a Riding man named Percy Johnson and the Assistant Instructors were Acting Sgts. Laurence Byford and Colin Sampson. The names of both the latter two will be well known to all Police Officers in the UK because they both went on to become HM Inspectors of Constabulary. Laurence Byford I think was also the first serving Police Officer to be called to the Bar. All three were super chaps and great Instructors.

We had a lot of fun both on and off duty on the course. We three Colonials drove Archie Dove mad with our tales of 'daring do' in the Colonies and when it came to the 'End of Course Banquet' he produced an excruciatingly funny long poem he had written about us.

There were of course the usual number of wags in the class and one of them, a D/Sgt from Lincolnshire used to have us in stitches taking off Percy Johnson who had a very exaggerated manner of speaking. Came the day of course when Percy caught him.

Our Class comprised mainly Inspectors and Sergeants from UK Police Forces but there was a sprinkling of Colonial Officers in it. The three of us, a chap from the Hong Kong Police and three or four blacks from the Cameroons and Nigeria. Also, sitting next to me was a Punjabi, a very nice chap named Aswalia, wearing a turban of course and when we exchanged personal details, he told me his Rank was Deputy Inspector General and asked me how many men I had under me in my last command. I said about fifty and asked him how many he had. He calculated for a while, aloud in Punjabi and said, "Seventeen million". I was of course astounded so much that he took out a piece of paper and did his calculation again. The figure was actually one hundred and seventy thousand! I was still astounded but he assured me that this was correct. It turned out that he was a very top man from the Indian Police Service and certainly the equivalent of the Commissioner of Police of the Metropolitan. I couldn't understand what he was doing amongst a bunch of Sgts. and Inspectors and mentioned it to Percy Johnson at the first opportunity. Major panic!! Nobody had realised the seniority of this chap who had thought the course would benefit him and had simply got his Force to apply like any other candidate. He was swiftly removed from the course and whisked off to meet the Chief Constable and visit the Home Office. I don't know what happened to him thereafter. He was there long enough though to be included in the Course Photograph which I still have.

The black Officers were at a distinct disadvantage and whilst it was obvious that they could learn sections of law parrot fashion, they were quite unable to apply them to situations. There were two senior Classes, 'A' and 'B' and two junior Classes. In addition there were two Classes composed totally of black Sgts and Inspectors from Uganda and Tanganyika. They were in junior Classes designed especially for them and when we had the entire School together, they were woefully out of place. We had a lot of laughs watching them when the snow and ice came because they were totally incapable of handling it and spent most of the time outside on their bottoms! They felt the cold awfully and usually wore overcoats, scarves and gloves even in class. Really, and I say this sincerely, what an upset for somebody undoubtedly borne in a mud hut!

We found the course very stimulating and informative and strangely for the Colonials, not too difficult because we had much more serious crimes under our belts than many of our English colleagues. I doubt very much whether there was a single man there who had dealt with half as many murders as I had. An interesting aspect which puzzled my Colonial colleagues and me was when we came to what the Instructors called, "The dirty fortnight!". This was crime involving sex and including all possible aspects. We were amazed to hear our black colleagues in class express total amazement and disgust when we came to buggery and bestiality. They claimed that such crimes were abhorrent to them and unheard of in Africa. We knew without a shadow of doubt that a great deal of this went on. You have only to speak to somebody with any experience of an African gaol, anywhere but it was not uncommon to catch two males at it in quiet spots outside a village, and in the larger cities such as Salisbury, Johannesburg and Lusaka etc., "drag" prostitutes could be seen about the streets after dark. Their patrons were other blacks as well and so the exclamations of our black colleagues met with much derision from us. Lesbianism amongst blacks was very uncommon then and of course it was never a crime.

I found that my memory skills had not diminished at all whilst I was away in the bush and I was easily able to absorb and remember the lessons each day. I had developed certain other interests in Doncaster, my home town which was only seventeen miles away and each night, after the evening meal back in our "digs", I would be off in my Peugeot to enjoy the delights of "Donny", often returning around one or two in the morning. My colleagues meanwhile had to spend two or three hours a night studying before popping off to the Pub for a pint before retiring. The fact that I never joined them and also didn't seem to study did not pass unnoticed and somebody put the boot in for me.

After Final Examinations we spent the last week having interviews with the Commandant and finishing off. The Commandant was a Chief Superintendent named Hainesworth, from the West Riding, (due to his white hair no doubt, being nick-named "The White Rabbit"). He was a bit of a stickler and very dry and when it came to the time for my interview with him, I was surprised to find myself the recipient of a lecture on self-indulgence and the need to buckle down and work. Since he terminated the interview by telling me that I had come third in the entire senior Course of two classes, I found his words especially difficult to justify. I never found out what he said on my report back to the Nyasaland Police but my superiors could only have been pleased that one of their chaps came third, ahead of all the UK Officers!

Chapter Twenty-Four

Back to Nyasaland

With three months in the middle of my leave being on a course, six months seemed to flash by and before I knew it I was on the Pendennis Castle, with my new car in the hold returning to Nyasaland via Cape Town. It was the first time I had done the trip by ship and I found it quite interesting but I did it a number of times subsequently and it became quite boring for me. The activities were not of my kind and lying sunbathing for a large portion of each day was definitely not my scene. One interesting feature which became apparent to me after a couple of voyages was what a small place East and Central Africa really was as far as people were concerned. It seemed to me that on any given voyage, I would have acquaintance with at least half the passengers who came from the Rhodesia, Nyasaland, Bechuanaland, Swaziland, Basutoland and even the East African Colonies. A similar statement used to be made about the 'Ulundi Passage' in the Royal Hotel in Durban. The Royal, was, and is, a magnificent five star Hotel and very plush. In those days however it was still very Colonial and through the entire hotel, from the front on Smith Street, to the rear ran a wide passage scattered with tables and easy chairs. It was a very pleasant and cool spot to have a lunchtime drink or indeed lunch. It was said that if you sat in that passage for long enough, everybody you knew in Africa would walk past you. I never put it to the ultimate test but I certainly saw many people I knew from all over Southern Africa as I sat there. The passage survives today in a somewhat altered form but its name is remembered in a very smart Bar named "The Ulundi".

I landed in Cape Town at the end of March 1961 just as South Africa declared itself to be a Republic, quite apart from the UK, and the currency was changed from the Pound to the Rand. I had never visited the country before and I had to say that the view as dawn came up and we entered Table Bay was one which I will never forget. I was lucky in later life to live there for twenty-eight years. My car was off-loaded and had to be "de-greased" before I could take delivery of it. In those days, to protect the cars en-route by Sea, they were sprayed with paraffin wax and had to be specially treated to get it off before they could be driven away. I still had some leave left to me and so set off to drive the long way back to Nyasaland. I gave a lift to a Northern Rhodesia Police Inspector who had been on the boat with me. We drove along the south coast of South Africa along what is now known as the "Garden Route", through Port Elizabeth and East London to Durban. Thence to Johannesburg and up to the Southern Rhodesian border at Beit Bridge and over the Limpopo. Then through Bulawayo and up to the Victoria Falls. Over the Zambezi to Livingstone on the northern bank in Northern Rhodesia. Up the Great North Road to Lusaka, where I left Paddy, the Northern Rhodesian Police Officer. Then from Lusaka, to the Nyasaland Border at Fort Jameson/Manning and so back to Zomba in the south. A trip of several thousand miles but an immensely enjoyable way of learning more about the beautiful Continent on which I lived.

I was somewhat disappointed to learn in Zomba that I was to be posted to Limbe, part of the twin Township of Blantyre/Limbe and the commercial capital of the country. Limbe was a large Police Station with well over a dozen white Officers, including some of the remaining UK contingent and I was reduced, albeit promoted, to Senior Inspector, to being a shift Officer and dealing with urban crime again. I even had to work shifts again, something I thought I had left behind me in Maltby! From being the 'kingpin' at Kasungu, I was just one of a number and it didn't sit well with me because I have never really been a 'Team Person'. Nothing really of note occurred whilst I was in Limbe, only a few months anyway, but I did have to travel much further to get to some hunting. Which I did.

One memory however which sits with me is a very amusing one. I have mentioned before that the UK contingent were very new and unaccustomed to African ways. In Limbe was the Head Office of ITC, (The Imperial Tobacco Company). In fact they seemed to own half of Limbe, were the main supporters of the Club and benefactors to the Town in many ways. They had a very beautiful dam in the middle of their residential area, most ornamental and teeming with chambo, the tilapia fish I have mentioned before. The fishing there was for their own employees' benefit and it was very difficult for any other person to get permission to fish. Except that is for the Police who were made ex-Officio "Fishing Members". This was Colonial Fishing at its very best. One entered the grounds after showing one's Permit, through a barrier at which waited a host of little 'Piccanins', (African children), all thrusting through the car window tins of worms they had dug up vying to be "employed". Having picked on one with the juiciest worms, the car was driven on round the dam until the occupants found a spot at which they wanted to fish. All very beautiful I must add again. The piccanin meanwhile had been running round the edge of the dam until he caught up. On arrival at the decided spot, we would get our camp chairs out, sit at the water's edge with our rods already made up. Simply a small float with a little weight and a small hook on the end of the outfit. The procedure was to point the rod over your

Chambo

shoulder whereupon the piccanin would thread a worm onto the hook, "Inde Bwana" he would say. That is "Yes Bwana" and you would cast in. In very short time the float would disappear and you would strike gently and haul in a chambo of some one and a half to two pounds. You lifted the fish over your shoulder and the piccanin would take it off, put a new worm on for you and put the chambo in the boot of your car. You never touched the fish yourself! Tell a UK fisherman that story and he would laugh you out of sight. And to watch these UK Policemen, most of whom had never caught a fish before, sitting there like real Bwanas, catching fish "Colonial style" absolutely slayed me! It didn't stop me from fishing the same way however and we ate a lot of fish. Again, you took a boot load of fish home, perhaps ten or fifteen. Your cook boy would be waiting, take the lot into the kitchen, fillet them, cook a couple of fillets for your supper with chips and put the rest in the deep freeze for later. Of course he always got a couple of fish for himself. Talk about fishing at its very best!

Chapter Twenty-Five

Bvumbwe Police Station

After two or three months of this I was told that a new Police Station was being built at Bvumbwe, about ten miles out of Limbe on the road to Mlanje – a tarred road, and I was to be the Officer-in-Charge. I was told that in addition to my work at Limbe, which was lessened, I was to liaise with the Clerk of Works from the Public Works Dept. and eventually take possession of the Police Station and the new house for me which was being built nearby. I used to visit each day or so and meet the Clerk of Works by arrangement. It was a new experience for me and interesting. And of course, the Police Station and house were built to my own personal requirements, within the original plans.

Bvumbwe
From Wikipedia

Bvumbwe is a small village located 13 km South East of Blantyre on the Limbe-Cholo road.

Its main feature is the Bvumbwe Agricultural Research Station (BARS) which was established in 1940 principally aimed at assaying factors affecting the growth and production of Montana Tung. The programme of work was, however, expended in 1950 to include investigations into improvements of Dairy Farming and the production of Coffee, Fruits and Vegetables.

The Clerk of Works was a Yorkshireman named Norman Garbutt and he was a real character. A Contract Officer, not permanent as we were, brought out for a specific job and for a specific term. They spoke no Chinyanja and were not required to. Norman however had picked up a few words which he put to hilarious use. To tell this story I must explain that in Chinyanja, most negative statements end in "Iai", meaning "no". A further word necessary to this story is "palibe", meaning "there isn't or there aren't". As in "Palibe mkhaka Bwana iai" meaning "There is no milk Bwana". Garbutt came one day to check on some work and he went into the Officer Commanding's toilet, adjoining what would be my office. The toilet cistern had not been put in level and Garbutt climbed into the foreman responsible for this piece of work. Remonstrating with him in his best Chinyanja he said. "Iai, palibe f*****g cock-eyed lai!". I could not restrain my mirth but I have to say that the foreman got the message!

Eventually the Station was finished and I had to take receipt of staff, about twenty five Sergeants and Constables, establish systems and make myself known to the various farmers and village Headman in the area. I had a very pleasant stay at Bvumbwe which however was not without incident.

Not far from the Police Station, about seven or eight hundred yards away, was a farm owned by David Peterkins, a nominated Member of the Legislative Council which in fact ran the Country and passed Laws under the "Chairmanship" of the Governor. He was thus a person of some standing. On his farm he had a fairly small dam sporting excellent Black Bass fishing.

I was by this time an established hunter and fisherman and Peterkins gave me permission to fish his dam whenever I liked. So, when times were slack at the Station, I would take a rod which I kept in my office and walk over the fields to the dam and fish for an hour or two. If I received a phone call which the desk Sergeant deemed required my attendance, the Station Bugler would stand outside my office and blow a call on his bugle. I then had to leg it across the fields to answer the telephone! Colonial Policing at its best!

The area around Bvumbwe which I had to Police comprised mainly white owned farms, and there were between the farms, large tracts of land belonging to the Government and occupied by African villages and farmland. Crime was the usual offences against property, against people and poaching small game off the white farms. Much of the land there was still wild and undeveloped. Some of the white owned farms produced coffee which is grown on small trees which in turn are planted in rows along low ridges.

As the rainy season approached each year there would be dramatic build-ups with huge black clouds appearing, frequently accompanied by massive thunder and lightning. For several weeks this happened without any rain appearing and finally the rains would break and we would have torrential downpours. Lightning strikes were quite common and every year a number of people, ignorantly taking shelter under trees or being caught on high ground would be hit and killed.

One day I was in my house having lunch when one of these build-ups developed. I didn't pay much attention and it was obvious it wasn't going to rain. However there was suddenly the most almighty crack of lightning which lit up the entire area and the thunder was instantaneous. We all know that you are supposed to count the seconds between the lightning and the thunder to determine how far away the lightning is. There was no time lag so the lightning was right by me. After about fifteen minutes the telephone from the Police Station rang and the duty Sgt. told me that the lightning had hit a group of coffee pickers about four hundred yards from my house.

I went to the scene and discovered that a number of African males and females had been in a long line picking coffee beans when the lightning struck. Because they were standing on the ridge, part of which was also on elevated ground, the lightning, taking the shortest course as it always does, had hit those on the highest part. They had been flung several yards away and some of them had sustained quite severe burns. Unfortunately a young girl aged about eighteen years had been killed instantly. We took the injured to the nearby Clinic for treatment and the dead girl we took straight through to Blantyre to the Queen Elizabeth Hospital. Being a large Hospital there was in residence a permanent, trained Pathologist, Stan Pilbeam, with whom I had quite a lot of dealings then and in the future. He said he would carry out a PM immediately as he was not too busy and we took the girl into the mortuary. She was cyanosed, exhibiting "blueness" which is one of the signs of being electrocuted but the interesting thing was the effect of the lightning on the metal on her body. She had been wearing a wrap-around cloth which is pretty much the staple dress of African women in the bush and it had been fastened with what we would call a kind of kilt pin, like a very large safety pin, on her thigh. Around her neck she had been wearing a heavy, cheap white metal necklace. When Stan removed her clothing we saw that the kilt pin had been burned about two inches into her thigh and the necklace had totally melted and fused into one chunk, deeply embedded in her neck. Stan explained that the lightning, which in fact comes upwards from the ground, had entered her body through the kilt pin and left it through the necklace, on its way upwards to meet the answering charge from the sky. A sad and graphic illustration of the way in which lightning works, and a strong warning not to stand under tall objects or on high ground when lightning is around. Golfers are often hit in Africa whilst sheltering under the nearest tree during a storm.

I have often heard doubt expressed in the Press and by people as to the existence of ball lightning. Well, I can give evidence on oath as to its existence as can my whole family. I later lived in Limbe in a very nice residential area on top of a hill called 'B.C.A. Hill', just outside Limbe. We were very high and looked out across quite a few mountains towards Blantyre. My mother had just arrived on holiday from England and we were sitting in the lounge having a drink. It was just before the rains and therefore very hot and all the doors and windows were open. They were metal framed. Lightning was cracking all round and we were enjoying the spectacle and the noise when there was a mighty whooshing noise and a brilliant electric blue ball, slightly larger than a football, flew in through the open doorway. It hung there about five feet from the ground in the middle of the lounge, for how long I couldn't say, only seconds I'm sure. We sat there stunned and then it whooshed again and flew just as fast out of the door through which it had entered. It left a burning electric kind of smell which I am told is ozone. Seven or eight of us saw and heard this and we can all remember it vividly even to this day. So ball lightning does exist and I can only wonder what would have happened if one us had been standing in the way!

Chapter Twenty-Six

Nguluwe – Wild Pigs

Because Bvumbwe was quite heavily populated by both whites and the local villagers, there was little game in the area. Plenty of small buck, which made good eating, guinea fowl and francolin, all shotgun shooting. The villagers were however plagued by wild pig which regularly pillaged their maize fields, destroying a whole village's food for a year as did the elephants in Kasungu. Now that they had a Police Station in their area, they expected us to do something about the pigs, or 'Nguluwe' as they were called!

David Peterkins had a son, also called David, about my age and we used to hunt bird together. One day the villagers from a particular village came and said the pigs were destroying their maize with great regularity. They said they could take us to a field any night and guarantee that the pigs would come. The pigs "M.O." was to enter the field in the middle of the night at one end of a row of maize and work their way down the row. They would knock down each plant, which stood six or seven feet high and simply eat the top cob, i.e. the sweetest. The rest of the cobs on the stalk would be wasted and the plant would die. At the end of the row they would turn round and start back again doing the same thing.

David Peterkins and I worked out that if we went early into the middle of the field, wearing headlamps and carrying shotguns loaded with LG shot, we could sit in darkness and wait for the pigs to work their way up to us. On a given signal we would switch on our lamps and let go with the shotguns on the pigs, which by this time would be upon us. I should mention that these pigs can go to three or four hundred pounds and the males carry massive tusks. They are very belligerent. Especially if they are being hunted! Strange attitude!

So we set the scene, went to the field pointed out by the villagers and worked our way into the middle of the field. We sat down on the ground between the rows, about ten yards apart and waited. The suspense was killing and every little night noise was amplified. Eventually, after about three hours we heard what was undoubtedly the pigs entering the field on the far side. The wind was in

The African Wild Pig

our favour so we thought we were in. It took ages for them to work their way into our vicinity and we began to hear them clearly snuffling, grunting and presumably talking to each other. When we judged, by their smell and the proximity of the noise, that they were indeed amongst us, we switched on our headlamps. A very grave miscalculation on our part for we had not realised that in the dense maize, with its very long broad leaves, our lights would simply be reflected back into our own eyes! There was utter pandemonium and chaos and the noise was unreal! Many, many pigs, all around us, squealing and screaming and making for the high ground. We didn't get a single shot off and in fact barely saw any pigs although they were all around us. The 'Adrenalin Rush' was incredible and we were both very frightened, packed up and went home to the safety of our beds. The villagers were very disappointed and we promised to devise another plan.

Incidentally, although I have shot a great deal in Africa I have very rarely been charged by an animal. One of the few occasions was a big boar which I shot near Liwonde. I knew I had hit it because I knocked one of its tusks out and the tusk was lying on the ground where the pig had been. We found a blood spoor which lead towards a thick patch of long grass about a hundred yards away. We tracked slowly along the spoor and when we were about thirty yards from the long grass, the pig suddenly burst from cover screaming and making straight for us. I was about to take a shot at it when it dropped in its tracks stone dead. What a relief, and what another 'Adrenalin Rush'!!

We had promised the villagers in Bvumbwe that we had not abandoned their problems so I organised a different approach. On a Sunday morning we had pig drives. Half a dozen of my friends would come from Blantyre and Limbe and we would go to a village which was being bothered by the pigs. We carried only shotguns because you cannot use a rifle at such close quarters as we would be. The villagers would assemble with saucepans or something metal they could bang and lots of dogs. Often twenty or thirty.

The pigs always spent their days in the bottom of deep river beds, or dongas as we called them. The undergrowth was very, very thick and provided excellent cover for them until nightfall when they could emerge and forage again. We used to find a pathway or a straight line of sight near the donga and the villagers would go in from the other side, banging their pans and drums and urging the dogs in front of them. We certainly used to get the pigs out and I was constantly amazed at the bravery of these nondescript little dogs. They would be totally unafraid and get hold of the pigs anywhere they could get a bite, and hang on. The pig were very, very savage, as they would be under circumstances like that and we used to lose one or two dogs every Sunday. The tusks would zip open a dog's ribs or stomach like a knife through butter. Eventually we usually managed to get a clear shot and kill the pig. A wounded escaped pig was frightful and we did our best to kill them on the spot. The dogs really came into their own when we had to track down a wounded pig. Anyway, we usually managed to get one or two and the villagers were satisfied, and also had meat because the pig wasn't bad eating. It was really 'wild pork'. My pig hunts became very popular and almost an event

One final incident from my life at Bvumbwe had a very comical side but which also resulted in my getting a Commendation from the Commissioner of Police. I was returning late one evening from the cinema in Limbe when I noticed a glow in the sky to the right of the road. Knowing there was high quality residential housing here I detoured and found myself at a large house which I later learned belonged to the General Manager of the FMB, a chap named Gale. The house was burning merrily along, the roof and the back half of the house was already almost destroyed. A number of neighbours and black Domestics were standing around just watching the house burn. I enquired if somebody could call the Blantyre/Limbe Fire Brigade and I also asked if there was anybody in the house but nobody knew. So I climbed in through a window in the unburned part of the house and did a quick search. I found three small children, all under the age of ten and all fast asleep, in their beds! I woke them, put on their dressing gowns and took them to the window through which I had climbed. I handed them through to neighbours and was of course glad they were safe. I don't believe that anybody expected they had been left by themselves in the house. In those days it was safe enough to do so from a crime point of view but still very unwise, as was proved. Since there was quite a lot of valuable furniture etc in the unburned part of the house, I busied myself in passing this through the windows also and got quite a lot out. I ceased this and beat a hasty retreat when one of the burning ceilings fell in around me, fortunately missing me!

At this time the town's single fire engine arrived, quite a modern Merriweather, manned by the Volunteer Firemen. There were no full time firemen in the country at that time. Ex-Officio, as Fire Chief, wearing a most distinctive white helmet with a huge Municipal Badge on it, was the Mayor, one Dillon Steyn. I am sure that if "London's Burning" had been invented, he would have seen himself as one of the chief characters in that. He took complete charge, ordering the others to unlimber their hoses, connect them up to the massive tanker which had followed the fire engine and position the hoses. He took the

lead on the most strategically positioned hose, much to the admiration of the crowd which had by now gathered, and shouted, "OK, let it go lads!". One of the firemen operated the pumps on the fire engine and they braced themselves for the flow. Nothing happened! Dillon Steyn shouted again, impatiently, to get the water flowing and when nothing happened still, abandoned his place on the lead hose and went to the fire engine to make sure the pumps were correctly switched on. They were - so he then, very importantly, climbed up on top of the tanker, opened a big manhole on the top of it and his head and shoulders disappeared inside. Immediately came this disembodied voice, echoing strangely, "There's no bloody water in here!". I must say, after all the build up and histrionics, I nearly died laughing. The tanker had to be sent off to a nearby stream to refill itself, meanwhile the house was burning away still. Eventually there was not much of it left and the fire was put out.

We all went home to bed and the next morning I went to work as usual. I had not been there long when the phone rang. Thank goodness I was not fishing because it was the Commissioner himself. Somebody in the crowd had thought fit to phone him and tell him the story and I got the usual, "Highest traditions of the Force", story with which I was of course pleased. Even more so a couple of days later when I got an Official Commendation.

From the Gales, never ever a word. Perhaps they were embarrassed about leaving their children!

Chapter Twenty-Seven

Chikwawa – Lower River

Chikwawa
(From Wikipedia)

Chikwawa is a town located in the Southern Region of Malawi. Set on the West bank of the Shire River, 50km South of Blantyre, it is the Administrative Capital of the Chikwawa District. The District covers an area of 4,755 km2.

The District lies in a Malaria Endemic area.

Shortly after this I received a promotion to Gazetted Rank and a transfer to Chikwawa on the lower Shire river. This was a much larger Station with over a hundred staff and a big area to patrol. To my delight, the Shire was a magnificent fishing river and Chikwawa was as good for game as had been Kasungu, albeit with only a tiny Game Reserve to protect the nyala, a beautiful antelope, very rare and shy. Chikwawa was also situated only twenty eight miles from Blantyre, up a massive escarpment which was often impassable in the rainy season, but very handy for shopping and entertainment and also a very, very hot area. The temperature often exceeded one hundred and ten Fahrenheit. As a result it was classed as a "hot" Station and "hot Station" hours were worked. We would start work in the morning at six o'clock and following the morning Parade carry on with normal duties. At 8am we went home for breakfast and returned at eight forty five until 1pm. Then everything packed in. This suited me because whilst the rest of the Boma used to have lunch and go and lie down under mosquito nets and a fan, I had the whole afternoon to go fishing or hunting, or to play tennis later when some of the younger Boma staff roused themselves. A very Colonial way of life!

The Boma staff comprised rather more than Kasungu had, having a District Commissioner, two Assistant D.C.s, and the full complement of PWD, Roads Staff, Agricultural Officers and so on. I also had two white Inspectors assisting me. There was no doctor, even though there was a large Hospital run by a senior Medical Aide and I think this was because of the close proximity of Blantyre.

The rare and shy Nyala

The District Commissioner was a very nice chap called Phillip Burkinshaw. An ex-Major in the Paratroopers who insisted on being called "Major Burkinshaw". One of his A.D.C.s had been a Major in some other Regiment and the third one of the triumvirate had been a Captain somewhere else. They all insisted in using their Military Ranks and I thought it a scream. When I popped in to see the DC for something or other, I always saluted him and said, "Corporal Bean reporting Sah!". He used to laugh but didn't seem to realise I was taking the "you know what!". He played a good game of tennis though!

The Machila

I must say here, that although most of the District Commissioners I knew were very decent chaps, their positions as the Queen's Representative in an area went rather to their heads. They did wield quite a lot of power.

Chikwawa sat on the Lower Shire River, which had wended its way down from Lake Nyasa and thence to Lake Palombe, thereafter cutting its way through Gorges until it got to the last Gorge, known as the Mpatamanga Gorge where it tumbled over the Murchison Falls to become the Lower River. This was about twenty miles up river from Chikwawa. It was a broad, very powerful river, typically African and it teemed with fish, hippo and crocodile, in places plenty of game came down to the river to drink also. After Chikwawa it continued down until the Elephant Marshes at Chiromo, a favourite duck shooting area and eventually joined the mighty Zambezi. In the old days, the river was navigable for fairly large boats and paddle steamers used to ply their way from Chinde on the coast up as far as Chiromo. Until the advent of the Railway from Beira this was the only way residents could enter Nyasaland. At Chiromo you took a kind of hammock called a Machila, slung between four porters who carried you up the escarpment! In my days there was still an old derelict paddle steamer moored at Chiromo. However, boats were not the only things to navigate their way up the Shire from the Zambezi. Tiger fish, (Hydrocynus vittatus), arguably the most powerful fighting fish in the world, worked their way up river until they got to the Murchison Falls above Chikwawa which they could not climb. They therefore congregated there and the fishing was superb. I spent many a happy afternoon up there, either by myself or with a friend, fishing off the rocks with big spinners on the end of forty pound steel trace, using fifteen or twenty pound line. The tigers' teeth, which were on the outer edge of their lips were interlocking and could easily cut through the steel trace. The method was to stand on a rock jutting out into the river, cast out as far as you could, forty or fifty yards, let the current, which was fast, take your line a couple of hundred yards downstream and then very slowly retrieve it. The current would spin the spoon. When you hit a tiger you felt as if you had snagged the bottom they hit so hard and they tail walked. To pull them in against the current required great effort and a lot of time. Commonly they came around six or seven

Tiger Fish

The Carmine Bee Eater

pounds although two weekends running in 1970 I broke the Nyasaland, (by then Malawi), record first with a fifteen pounder on fifteen-pound line and the next week with a sixteen pounder on eight-pound line. These were the only two fish over ten pounds caught that year and as far as I know, my record still stands. I actually caught these from a boat.

At Chikwawa the Boma houses stood on top of a hundred foot cliff and at certain times of the year, one could approach the edge of the cliff quietly and then clap one's hands and out of holes in the cliff face would stream thousands of carmine beeeaters. Most beautiful birds about the size of a starling, electric blue on the top and wings with a green head and a brilliant carmine chest and front. As the flock flew out it was a startling blue but as it wheeled and showed its underside, it changed to this beautiful scarlet. A fabulous sight and one which today I would have loved to photograph. I had to travel some distance to get from the Boma to a place on the river where I could fish so one day, surveying the cliff face, I saw a cleft which ran from the top to the water level, starting near the bottom of my garden. I borrowed about twenty prisoners from the Prison for a few days and they slowly converted the cleft to steps and built a platform at the water's edge. I then didn't have to travel far from my house to go fishing. Tiger were not so abundant here as up near the falls but I did catch them together with very large catfish called 'Vundu' which could commonly run to sixty or seventy pounds, my best being ninety five pounds. It was very pleasant fishing and my cook boy was instructed to run down the steps every hour or so with a cold Coca-Cola or later in the day, a cold Beer! Colonial style fishing again!

As far as hunting was concerned, we didn't get many elephant there, although there were a few, but lion and leopard, none of which I used to shoot, were there, and plenty of antelope of all kind. I didn't have to go more than a few miles from the Boma to find the smaller stuff but used to go over some hills to an area called Chapananga where I would camp overnight, for eland, buffalo and such. I mentioned before that I was only charged one or two times in my hunting career and Chapananga was one of them. A beautiful sable bull, now fully protected everywhere in Africa, got up after I had knocked it down and came straight for me. They have been known to kill lion so I was

African pulling out a Vundu

very apprehensive as it came towards me. However, about thirty yards from me I shot it again, full frontal and it went down dead. Big 'Adrenaline Rush' again!

Hippo created the same problem with the villagers, that the pigs had in Bvumbwe and the elephants had in Kasungu. They used to wreck the maize gardens and the villagers expected the local Police to put an end to their depredations. I used to go out with a couple of my African Police, or one of the more adventurous white Government Officers in the area and again wait for them to come in the middle of the night. Heart in the mouth stuff again as we heard them approach, but this time we were not in the middle of the field on the ground but up convenient trees. We got a couple but were not very successful. When we fired our guns they would take heed and make off and not come back for a couple of nights, but the maize was too sweet for them to resist and they would soon be back. You may wonder what happened to them when we did shoot them. The villagers ate them and what they couldn't eat immediately, they dried into what in Africa is called "Biltong" and in America, "Jerky".

There was a great deal of witchcraft on the Lower River and whilst I was there, two separate burnings at the stake occurred. Women, smelled out as witches and receiving the traditional treatment. We never caught the people or the witchdoctors responsible as they were too well concealed. We had many deaths from Mwabvi poisoning and again rarely caught the witchdoctors. They either came across the border from P.E.A. and quickly went back or the villagers refused to identify them. The victims were identified as witches by the Ngomas, (witchdoctors), perhaps because all the chickens in one village died, or the rains didn't come, or the maize didn't grow properly. Or perhaps a person died for no good reason and a witch was considered responsible. The Ngoma would be called out and the 'Smelling Out' Ritual would commence.

Other crimes were the usual, assaults, murders, poaching, housebreaking and so on. One "crime" I remember particularly from Chikwawa was the illegal beating of drums! I see or hear them now on the television and I laugh, but in most of Africa, for white people it was no laughing matter. As soon as a batch of illegal booze had been distilled, out would come the drums thereby attracting customers from far and wide to buy it. This often resulted in fights, murders now and again, rapes and all the crime associated with heavy drunkenness. The drums would go on all night and it was impossible to sleep. So a telephone call to the night duty Sgt. at the Police Station would be made. "Sgt. go out and find those drums and arrest the owners!". It was actually an offence to sound drums after a certain hour! Pathetic now I feel, but try living with it night-after-night before you judge.

Chapter Twenty-Eight

The Human Crocodile Murder

One late afternoon one of my Detective Sergeants came to me with a story which turned out to be probably the most important, or notorious case of my Police career and one which was subsequently written up in the world press.

I need briefly to describe the Lower Court system extant in Nyasaland in those days. We had the Resident Magistrate's Court which I have described earlier with a Professional Magistrate rather like the old Stipendiary Magistrates in the UK. In addition, at the same level although used less frequently was the District Commissioner's Court. Below that was the Court held by the Senior Local Chiefs, rather like the Small Claims Courts. It was called the "Local Court".

The Official Government Districts were divided up into the Chiefs' Areas and these were Tribally determined. The Senior Chief was a pretty important character and one the Government held in considerable regard. He had the power to hear minor assault cases, divorce or marry people, and perhaps most of his work was determining minor claims for damages or loss.

In this instance the D/Sgt. had been to the Court of Chief Chapanga, a pretty big Chief responsible for the Chapananga area. One in which I hunted very regularly. The Sgt. wanted to tell me about a case the Chief had heard that day in which a man named Elard Chipendale, claiming to have the powers to turn himself into a crocodile, (in fact a magic crocodile!), who had been paid by another man named Odreck Kasoci to kill a little girl aged eight years. The agreed price had been two Pounds ten shillings. This had taken place three years earlier and shortly after the killing took place, Elard was caught for burglary and served an eighteen month sentence in jail. Obviously a versatile kind of chap! The tale they both told and agreed upon was that Odreck identified the child to be killed and in due course, Elard entered the river where she and her friends bathed in the evening, changed himself into a crocodile, he swam up to her and grabbed her and made off down river with her. At this time the village Headman who had been returning from a hunting trip saw the "crocodile" taking the girl and let go both barrels of his shotgun. ('shotti-gun' as they were known). Twisting to avoid the shot, Elard, who had hold of the little girl's forearm, broke it. He made his getaway after drowning the child and met Odreck nearby, reporting the deed was done. Odreck then gave him ten shillings, which they called "Blood Money" as an advance on the whole fee to be paid very shortly. Elard shortly after went into the "Kingi Georgie Hotel", as prison was known to them, and when he had served his time, came looking for his balance of the fee. Odreck however twisted and turned on payment of the balance and eventually in desperation, Elard went to the Local Court and sued him for it! This whole story was recorded in the Court Record and they both signed it. Chief Chapanga said, "Fair enough, the money is due, pay it".

It was paid into the Court Funds, a receipt was issued and it was disbursed to Elard! An Official Government Receipt for a Murder Fee!

The Statements to the Chief's Court were freely offered and voluntary and as such sufficient evidence to commence enquiries. I immediately despatched the Sgt. back to Chapananga's Court with the instructions to seize the Court Record and bring in the two suspects. I read the Court Record with amazement because here I had a full confession to a murder without any suggestion of remorse or guilt.

"I am crocodile-man"—alleged confession

Cutting from 'The Nyasaland Times' with the photo captioned "Alleged Crocodile Man" Elard Chipendale (second left) and Odreck Kasoci (right) - both accused of murder - are escorted from the Blantyre High Court.' (Hand dated March 22nd 1963) [see end of Chapter for transcription of this article]

Once we had the two men in our custody we recorded full cautioned statements from both of them in which they repeated just about word for word what they had said in the Chief's Court. We then went out to the village concerned and recorded statements from the parents of the dead girl, other villagers who had witnessed the incident and the village Headman who had fired his shotgun at the "crocodile". None of these people knew anything about the two men being involved and indeed the "Crocodile Man" was not even known to any of them. Odreck was known to them but was no relation and indeed, we never ever discovered a motive for the contract killing! One vital point which did not come out from them, was the fact that Elard, whilst in the water, had broken the little girl's arm. Nobody had noticed it when her body was recovered or when she was buried.

We obtained an Exhumation Order and went out to the village burial ground together with my colleague Stan Pilbeam, the Pathologist from Blantyre. I probably conducted about a dozen exhumations during my time in Nyasaland and some of them were pretty grim. Villagers had to be pressed into service to open up the grave and of course we had to have somebody present to identify the grave and the body in it. The villagers were very reluctant to assist us and in some cases, were actively belligerent to the extent that we had to have armed Policemen standing by.

This was not a problem in this case however and we duly opened the grave. She had been buried on a very sandy hillside three years previously and the body had completely disintegrated. Only dry bones remained and these had drifted some way from each other due to movement of the ground. We had to use a fine sieve to discover what bones we could and did in fact manage to get virtually the whole skeleton with, most importantly, the broken bones from the girl's forearm.

The importance of this will now be seen as the only corroboration for the two confessions. Under English Law, and Nyasaland Law also, a man cannot be convicted of murder purely on the strength of his own confession. In this case the broken bones provided the corroboration as only the "Crocodile Man", Elard, had knowledge of this.

Both men were then charged with murder and in their reply to the charge, once more repeated their whole stories. So that was three identical confessions from each man. They were committed for trial and eventually the case came up before the Chief Justice, Spencer-Wilkinson, in the High Court in Blantyre. Word of the case had got outside Nyasaland and a number of international reporters attended the trial. Only one word can describe the trial and that is 'bizarre'! There was no jury trial in Nyasaland but the Judge sat with three Assessors who were Elders of the tribe to which the accused persons belonged. They had no legal standing but were there to advise the Judge on matters of tribal law and custom. The accused exhibited no concern at their plight and there were some very funny moments in the trial. One in particular occurred when the Crown Counsel prosecuting asked Elard how he became a "Magic Crocodile". He replied that he had been shown the art by an uncle who was also a "Crocodile Man". He said that to make himself into a crocodile, he dressed himself in the bark of a certain tree and uttered an incantation. The Counsel asked him to demonstrate this to the Court and you could almost hear an audible gasp from the black audience as they expected to see an immediate transformation. He said, of course, he couldn't do it in Court so Counsel asked him if he saw other crocodiles when he was in the water and what their reaction to him was. He said that when he was in the water he was 'brothers' with the other crocodiles and conversed with them in crocodile language! Counsel asked him for a demonstration of crocodile language and he said he could only do it when he was in the water. The white spectators of course broke up laughing but I am quite certain that the majority of the black people present believed the man to be able to change into a crocodile!

When all the evidence was heard the Judge asked the Assessors what was their opinion of the matter. The first replied, "This girl was killed by magic!". The second said, "This thing was a magic thing!". and the third said, "This was a magic crocodile!". I doubt very much if this influenced the Judge in any way and he duly sentenced them to death and they were hanged in Zomba Prison later. Apart from the bizarre nature of the case, it was unusual in that there was so little hard evidence against them. They were never identified by anybody as being suspected of a crime, indeed the villagers had always believed the girl died from a crocodile attack, a very common cause of death in the area. Had they pleaded "Not Guilty" instead of being so willing to tell their story, I wonder if the case would have stood up. Had they not gone to Court to settle their civil case, nobody would ever have known about it. And as I have said, we never uncovered a motive for the killing nor even a connection between Odreck and the family.

I have mentioned that most of the black people in Court believed quite sincerely that Elard was indeed capable of turning himself into a crocodile so I thought that at my next Monday morning Parade in Chikwawa, which was followed by a talk on some aspect of law, I would talk about witchcraft in a naive attempt to convince my Policemen that it didn't exist. I opened the meeting by reminding them of the crocodile case and to get them going said, "I expect that if one of you is walking down the Police Lines, (the residential area in their Camp), on a moonlight night and you feel a touch on your shoulder, you think it is a 'Tokoloshe', (a little devil!). They pooh-poohed this idea and said that it would be one of their friends playing a trick on them. I thought I was getting somewhere and went on to ask if on a full moon any of them had seen their grandmothers riding on the back of a hyena? (A popular belief). Again they pooh-poohed me so I thought I had got my Policemen well along the path to civilisation until one of them said, "Not a hyena Bwana, a lion!", the others all nodded their heads in agreement and I could only shake mine in frustration. You will never stop Africans believing in witchcraft, not even today!

Transcript of Newspaper Article
"I am Crocodile-Man" – Alleged Confession
Blantyre, Thursday.
Police and Native Court Officials alleged in the Nyasaland High Court here today that an African told them he had disguised himself as a crocodile and killed a young African girl for £4 10s.
They were giving evidence at a murder trial in which Elard Chlpandale ls accused of dragging eight-year-old Mponda Simenti into the Mwanza River and killing her. Also accused of murder is the chlld's grandfather, Odreck Kasoci, who ls alleged to have employed Elard because he believed he was a "Crocodile Man". Both men have denied the charge.
The trial is before the Chief Justice of Nyasaland, Sir Edgar Unsworth, sitting with three African Assessors. Mr. T.J.C. Joseph appears for the Crown, Mr. R.G. Topping for Elard; and Mr. M.B. Mehta for Odreck.
When the trial opened yesterday the Crown alleged that in March, 1959, Odreck offered

Elard a sum of money to kill Mponda. After the girl had been killed, Odreck had refused to pay the full amount. When Elard returned to the village three years later he is said to have complained to the Native Court where he was awarded £2 10s. The civil case was heard by a Policeman who reported the matter and both men were arrested.

Today, the Clerk of the Native Court, Abbas Matenje, produced the Court Record. He read Odreck's evidence in which he is alleged to have eventually admitted the arrangement, but said the money involved was £2 10s., not £4 10s.

Village Headman Chikweo said he was a Councillor during the civil hearing, and alleged that Odreck had admitted employing Elard to kill the child.

DISOBEDIENT

Chikweo said he understood Odreck had asked Elard to kill the child, "because she was disobedient". Later this evidence was ordered to be disregarded as "hear-say."

Dr. S.T. Pilbeam produced a small cardboard box containing the child's bones which, he said had been exhumed last year. He was unable to say how the child had died. Detective Sergeant Kusiyana said he was present at the Native Court when Elard demanded the money. Both men were later arrested. Elard had made two statements. Sgt. Kusiyana alleged. In one Elard said: "I went to the river, I found the child with other children. I went to the children and seized the child. I took her down to the river. People saw me and the Headman fired at me. I broke her arm and stabbed her twice".

In the second Alleged Statement he repeated that he killed the child because Odreck asked him to. Sergeant Kusiyana said Odreck made an alleged statement in which he said: "It is true what Elard said. I told him to kill my grand-daughter and he killed her."

The trial was adjourned until tomorrow.- Sapa.

Chapter Twenty-Nine

Portuguese Neighbours Again

Chikwawa had a border contiguous with P.E.A. on its southern side and on occasion whilst hunting, I believed that I might have strayed across the border which was of course not delineated in any way. Once, in the distance I had seen what I thought was a Portuguese Army truck and hid behind a tree not wishing to be put in a Portuguese Jail for illegal entry. I had a sub-Station under an African Inspector named Chungwa. He was very intelligent and educated and went on later to much higher things in the Force. He used to tell me that at the far end of his area there was a little used track which actually went through the bush into P.E.A. until it met up with quite a large road. I decided to investigate this track and one day, after Chungwa had found a local villager who professed to know the way, set off in the Land Rover. We followed what could hardly be described as a track for several miles until the villager announced that we were now in P.E.A. How he knew, I don't know. The track soon widened out until it met a very large, well maintained dirt road. We followed this road until we came to quite a large town which we learned was called Mutarara and was an Administrative Headquarters. We found our way to the Administrative Offices and asked to see the Administrador. We were ushered into a beautifully appointed air-conditioned office and met by a Portuguese man dressed in immaculate whites. He spoke perfect American English and expressed great surprise at seeing us. When I explained that I was the Officer-in-Charge of his neighbouring District across the border he became very excited and welcoming.

He closed his office and took us to his house just outside the town where he lived in a mansion with dozens of servants who were under the command of his wife. He had learned his English in the Azores which at that time were still Portuguese Possessions and was in charge of a huge District which stretched all the way to the Zambezi. He had many white Portuguese Troops under his command. It was about mid-morning when we arrived and I was somewhat surprised, although I shouldn't have been, when he included Chungwa in everything we did and talked about. He obviously assumed that Chungwa was an "Assimilado". I just wasn't accustomed to sitting down with black people – not that I minded at all.

His wife produced a magnificent array of cakes and refreshments with coffee and we enjoyed a long discussion about each other's situation and way of life. It soon got near lunchtime and his wife came in and rattled off something in Portuguese and he asked us if we would stay for lunch. We had written off the day so we accepted quite happily and continued chatting.

In due course a drinks trolley came in and he started plying us with Manica Beer, a quite potent local Lager, Chungwa also!

Then this was followed by a larger trolley on which there was a huge display of what you might call today "Antipasta". Many contents of which I had never seen before. We tucked in and the Manicas continued to appear, (I wasn't supposed to be a drinker at that time).

It got to about 2 o'clock and I was thinking of making a break for it when his wife came in again and nodded to him whereupon he said, "Shall we have lunch now!". I was stunned – and full – and not totally sober! We had no choice but to go into his dining room and sit down to a repast which had about eight courses. The main course was roast porcupine, which he had shot a couple of days earlier. I am always a little reluctant to try new dishes but had no choice this time, not wishing to offend our host. I found it quite pleasant and a cross between chicken and pork.

In my time in Africa I have eaten many unusual meats, virtually all the antelope, buffalo, hippo, crocodile tail and elephant trunk. The latter was at the Monomatapa Hotel in Salisbury and I was somewhat put off by the round piece of what looked like steak, with two round holes in the middle of it. I was told that these were the nostrils! Not for the weak stomachs!

He had really pushed the boat out and promised to return our visit. He asked if he could traverse my area to go and do his shopping in Blantyre as it was his closest thing to a shopping centre. Probably about sixty miles from Mutarara going through Chikwawa and of course I agreed. I arrived home about eight in the evening, bloated with food and Manicas and very tired after a full day. Most entertaining though.

It wasn't long after this that I was woken early one morning by my houseboy who informed me that there was a Portuguese Bwana wanting to see me. It was my friend and he had several boxes of fresh vegetables which he had grown and brought for me. I didn't and don't eat vegetables but they were very welcome amongst the rest of the Boma.

He told me that he had taken a Road Gang and for several weeks worked on his little road into Nyasaland and that if I went there I would find it to be quite a large well maintained road now. This was ostensibly so that he could go shopping in Blantyre but I realised that around that time the Portuguese in P.E.A. were becoming increasingly twitchy, hence the large numbers of troops in his area, and in fact the road represented his bolt-hole should he ever have to flee. In fact this actually happened in some places but I don't know whether my friend ever had to use his. He used to come across about once a month and would never stay for a meal, thank goodness as I couldn't compete with his set-up, and always brought vegetables with him, occasionally a haunch of venison he had shot.

Chapter Thirty

Swimming with Tigers!

One final adventure, nearly resulting in my death, occurred whilst I was at Chikwawa. I was the local expert on tiger fishing and people would phone from Blantyre or come and see me for advice.

One Sunday two friends from Blantyre came down to fish with me. One was David Peterkins, my old pig shooting friend from Bvumbwe and the other an Agricultural Officer named Mike Perkins. We went to my usual spot at the foot of the falls and took up our positions on convenient rocks jutting out into the current. At this point the white water came rushing down the narrow gorge and poured out into a very wide section of river. The main force of the water continued down the left hand side of the river but about four hundred yards from the foot of the falls part of the current peeled off to the right and ran in a huge circle, the full four hundred yards, back to the foot of the falls. It was almost like a vast, very slow moving whirlpool. David Peterkins' tackle became stuck on a rock about six feet in front of him, under water. What he didn't know, and I never knew why this happened, the water used to ebb and flow as much as six feet in a couple of minutes. Suddenly David's tackle became clear of the water and he stepped forward to clear it. As he reached it, the water surged again, lifted him off his feet and whisked him away down stream. I was not unduly alarmed as he was not in the white water but in the slow moving part of the river. I shouted to him just to tread water and the circular current would bring him round full circle and near the bank where he could climb out. He heard me and went off almost gaily downriver. About two hundred yards down however he threw his arms up, shouted and went under water. The water was much too fast for crocodiles to be there and the hippo were further downriver. In any event they would not have attacked in the water. He came up again and shouted that he was in a whirlpool and couldn't get out. Mike Perkins said, "You are a good swimmer Christopher. Go and get him". Without any thought I immediately dived off the rock I was on and struck off down stream.

When I was about fifty yards from him, David suddenly reappeared and the whirlpool disappeared, part of this mysterious ebbing and flowing I spoke of. As I had suggested, the current then took him round the circle and when he got near Mike, he was able to pull him out.

I then set out across the pool to make the flow near the bank. When I got about twenty yards from the two of them I was suddenly caught in another current which held me in one spot I couldn't get forward to them or move backwards. They started panicking and casting their lines to me but in their haste could get nowhere near me. I was beginning to tire now in the strong water and feared that if I was taken into the white water I would not be strong enough to fight it. Just as suddenly, the current holding me disappeared and I was able to move forward to the bank where they pulled me out. We were very shaken, two of us had nearly drowned and we sat very quietly for some time before we started fishing again. We didn't tell many people about this feeling somewhat stupid about the whole thing. About five years later David died, a young man, from Cancer of the stomach.

Chapter Thirty-One

Chileka Police Station

Out of the blue, about eight months before the end of my then current Tour, I was again transferred, this time to Chileka. The Police area was smaller but more important than Chikwawa in that about half a mile from the Police Station was Chileka International Airport, in fact the only International Airport in Nyasaland at that time. Amongst my other duties I was responsible for its security. There was a much smaller black

Chileka
(From Wikipedia)

Chileka is located nine miles (16km) West of the Commercial Capital City of Blantyre, (the largest City in the Country) in the Southern District of Malawi.

It's main facility is Chileka Intarnational Airport, the only one situated in the South of the Country.

population but many more white people, mainly employees at the Airport and our houses were situated on the end of, (magic!), a tarred road leading from Blantyre, which was ten miles away, to the Airport. There were many pleasures associated with being stationed at Chileka because for a start, we could do all our shopping at any time without having to take a day off and travel. There were cinemas, (two), and two Sports Clubs and I was able to play squash again at a Court about five miles from home.

The Airport people were a very pleasant bunch and I formed a lot of friendships, some of which survive to this day. The Airport Manager, "Jacko" Jackson was a real character and I was always welcome in his office for a coffee and a joke. The first daily occurrence of any note was the midday arrival of the Central African Airways, (C.A.A.), Viscount from Salisbury. I was always present in the doorway of the Ground Staff office when it arrived – for two reasons. I soon got to know all the Pilots and one of them would hand me that morning's Rhodesian Herald Newspaper, the daily paper from Salisbury. I was thus the first person in the whole of Nyasaland to receive my daily paper which I could take home and read over lunch. On all my previous Stations, my Rhodesian Heralds were at least a week old when I received them. The other reason I was waiting in the doorway was of a rather more venal nature. These were the days when air hostesses were picked as much for their looks as anything else and the CAA girls were not lacking in this respect. Some of them had even been Beauty Queens and models. Having been starved of female pulchritude for so many years in the bush, it was a great pleasure to watch the two Hostesses of the day walk from the plane to the office where I was standing. The pilots were usually the last off the plane but on some days you could watch both pilots scramble off the plane quickly and make for the office to join me. I soon learned why. One of the hostesses, a girl named Wendy Shed, was especially outstanding and had been Miss Copperbelt a few

Chileka International Airport

years before. Apart from being stunning, she had the most amazing swaying walk and the pilots' rush to join me was purely so they could also watch her walk from the plane! For some reason she was known in CAA as "Tool Shed!" I can't imagine why!

Some five or six years after I left Chileka there occurred an incident in which I was very happy not to be involved. A South African Airways 737, shortly after taking off from Salisbury Airport in Southern Rhodesia was hi-jacked by three Arabs, lead by one known as "Mad" Fred Hamil. They hi-jacked the plane because they believed that Harry Oppenheimer was on board en-route to Mauritius. The pilot convinced them that he didn't have enough fuel to fly to Mauritius without refuelling at Chileka and they allowed him to land. Once the plane was on the ground at Chileka and they realised they didn't have Oppenheimer as a captive, after lengthy negotiation they allowed the passengers to disembark but made the crew stay on board in the hope they would be refuelled and could take off for points unknown. This took place on a Monday or a Tuesday, certainly the beginning of the week.

There is only one main runway at Chileka and the plane was parked near the end of the runway. In those days there was one weekly international flight from London when a VC10 belonging to British Airways terminated its flight on a Friday and returned to Heathrow. The runway could not be used at this time because of the 737 blocking it. This particular week also the President, Dr. Hastings Banda was due to fly to London from Chileka and the world looked on with interest to see how the situation would be dealt with. Nobody was allowed to stand in Banda's way, not even "Mad" Fred. Negotiations failed to produce any results and on the Friday morning about four hours before the VC10 was due, orders came down from the President's Office that all white personnel were to be cleared from the Airport vicinity and the Police Mobile Force went in. Without further ado they raked the plane from end to end with automatic weapons and in no time "Mad" Fred and Co. appeared in the doorway with their hands above their heads. They were of course arrested and tried but I cannot remember what happened to them. I do know however that the 737 was almost a write-off as a result of the small arms fire. The fuselage was riddled with bullet holes and the plane had to be flown back to Johannesburg at about ten thousand feet because it could not be pressurised. S.A.A. Were not impressed with the Malawi Security Forces!

The VC10 of course landed on time and Banda appeared with his retinue – and departed for London on time. Being a dictator at least ensures your planes leave on time!

Chapter Thirty-Two

Internal Self-Government and The Ice Cream Boys

These halcyon moments passed however and we soon became embroiled in the arrangements for the first Internal Elections in which all citizens of Nyasaland had a vote. There were a number of political parties but the biggest by far was the Malawi Congress Party. It still is. This was the old "A.N.C." and was lead by Dr. Hastings Banda. The run-up to the elections followed the usual route for elections in Africa. Thousands of incidents of intimidation and assaults to persuade the general public to vote for Dr. Banda as he then was known. He was, as I have said, a Medical Doctor. The various parties had lots of rallies and would ride around Blantyre/Limbe in their trucks with loads of supporters and banners on the back. The whites had many a laugh at the MCP supporters because they selected as their emblem a black cockerel against a rising sun. Their battle cry was "Ufulu", (Freedom), the same word as in East Africa although there it was "Uhuru". These trucks would rattle round Blantyre causing great disruption whilst the supporters cried "Vote for Dr. Banda and his Black Cock!". I swear this is true and of course the whites loved it! The blacks never understood why the whites, who were totally opposed to Banda, used to cheer and give the thumbs up whenever they heard the cry.

The MCP of course won the election with a landslide victory, nobody dared vote for anybody else and I doubt if even today rural blacks understand that a secret ballot is just that. They were told by the intimidators outside the Polling Booths that they, the intimidators would know who the voter voted for and he would be beaten up, if not killed, did he not vote for the MCP. I saw Independence elections subsequently in Bechuanaland and Southern Rhodesia and they followed exactly the same pattern.

Anyway, The MCP were voted in and Banda became the first Prime Minister. He immediately, in common with all subsequent black Presidents/ Prime Ministers, developed a huge entourage which accompanied him whenever he set out on any road. Traffic in Blantyre soon became completely snarled up when the motorcade approached and because it often didn't have a clear run, an order was issued from the Office of the PM to the effect that when the motorcycle outriders in front of his entourage came into sight, all traffic must pull in to the side of the road and wait until the procession passed. This did not go down at all well with the normal law abiding citizens of the town, especially the whites. Banda had by this time established a branch of the Youth League of the MCP as his "Young Pioneers". These were in fact nothing more than a bunch of thuggish bodyguards, numbering more than a couple of hundred in Blantyre. They were dressed in long white coats and became known as "The Ice Cream Boys". If the road was not cleared fast enough for their satisfaction, they started stopping the white motorists, dragging them from their cars and administering severe beatings. There were some very unpleasant incidents which involved hospitalisation, some of which were actually committed in front of Police Officers. Since it was not law to stop for the cavalcade, and in any event, the assaults were not justified, in a lot of cases the culprit "Ice Cream Boys" were arrested and put in the cells. Within a couple of hours an instruction would come from the PM's office that the "Ice Cream Boys" were to be released. Quite obviously the various Officers-in-Charge refused to release them as they were guilty of often serious assault. Within a day, official orders to release would come down from the office of the Commissioner of Police. This went down very badly with honest Police Officers trying to uphold the law and protect members of the public and of course, the public themselves were incensed that they could be attacked with clear impunity.

Feelings began to run very high and whilst I would not say that rebellion in the Police was imminent, there was great disquiet amongst the senior Officers as they could see that it was becoming impossible for them to perform their duties without political interference. The Commissioner, John Mullens, a very nice gentle chap with whom I used to play squash, was obliged to call a meeting of the senior Officers in the Southern Province at Divisional Police HQ. He was clearly carrying out instructions, presumably emanating from Whitehall and he told us that we were going through difficult times(!) and that we must do all we could to accommodate these emerging politicians. He finished his address with the words, "We must all bend over backwards to ensure Independence arrives smoothly!". There was an uproar amongst the Officers present especially when he said that none of the "Ice Cream Boys" were to be arrested in future, whatever they had done, without his express authority. Well, what Police Officer worth his salt could work under restrictions like that?

A number of us went back to our Stations and submitted our requests for early retirement under the "Golden Handshake" system. This of course pleased Whitehall because at this time they started phasing out the white Officers in all spheres of Government Service. At first, the time I am speaking of, people were welcome to submit a request for voluntary retirement but as time went along, it started to be compulsory. There were very generous compensation schemes set up and I eventually walked out with a small Pension, a third of which I had commuted for cash, a lump sum of twelve thousand Pounds in compensation for losing my career, and a two thirds Pension which although at that time was not very much, I was only twenty seven years old, when I reached the age of fifty five, it increased by 1050%! It always provided me with a nice little nest egg to spend whenever I visited the UK.

Chapter Thirty-Three

Early Retirement and the Fleshpots

So, there I was a retired Superintendent of Police at the age of twenty seven, with what was for that time a lot of money in my hands, on leave for eleven months with my full salary coming in. The world at my feet, but what was I going to do?

I flew down to Cape Town and embarked on the "Transvaal Castle", Union Castle's newest passenger vessel and set sail for Southampton. I watched Table Mountain disappear into the sunset and said "Goodbye" to Africa. Or so I thought!

I arrived back in Doncaster, and set about, without any haste, sending out job applications with my C.V. To my increasing disappointment, although I was a very highly trained Police Officer with every kind of course and experience under my belt, nobody wanted to know me! I sent out probably some two hundred applications and in only a mere handful did I get any acknowledgement at all. All my experience was of no use on the UK market plus it was quite flooded with ex-Colonials as Britain got rid of her Colonies as fast as she could.

I decided, reluctantly, to go back to South Africa and try my luck there. The short time I had spent in Cape Town had persuaded me that it could be a beautiful place in which to live. I took the "Pendennis Castle" back to Cape Town with my new Ford Zephyr on board and put myself up at a five star Hotel, "The Majestic" in Kalk Bay. I tried, in a somewhat desultory manner to find work in the Cape but failed. I must say, with a new car, plenty of money in my pocket and a steady monthly income by way of my salary which was still being paid, I didn't try too hard but rather enjoyed the fleshpots.

I then realised, with something of a jolt, that in a couple of months my salary was going to stop as my leave would come to an end. My lump sum had dwindled greatly also owing to my life style both in the UK and Cape Town so my thoughts went back to the Police Service again. Something I really was qualified to do.

I enquired of the Crown Agents if there were any surviving Colonies with vacancies for Police Officers and learned that there were vacancies in Bechuanaland, (now Botswana), Basutoland (now Lesotho) and Swaziland. I fancied Bechuanaland because I knew there were still vast quantities of game there and I could carry on my hunting.

The Administration of Bechuanaland at that time was carried out from what was called "The Imperial Reserve" in Mafeking, a small town in the Northern Cape best known for the Siege there in the Boer War. The Reserve was in fact a piece of land, owned, or leased by Britain, from the South African Government on which were situated all the Government offices and housing. It was on the main railway line and about twenty miles from the Bechuanaland border. It was also about a thousand miles from Cape Town and I thought that if I drove up there and saw the Authorities I could short circuit the system to obtain a post so I did this. To a certain extent I was correct in my thinking. I was welcomed by Colonel Bill Bailey, the Commissioner of Police who told me that I could be appointed as a Senior (Chief) Inspector without any delay, but he advised me to go back to the UK and sign on through the Crown Agents in order to qualify for expatriate terms of employment. These were much better in terms of pay, leave and transport to the UK at the end of a tour.

So back down the road to Cape Town, embarked on what was the final voyage of the "Athlone Castle" and back to Southampton, with my car again. My arrival in Southampton was not auspicious as the handlers managed to drop my car over the side of the boat whilst they were off loading. It suffered severe damage to the roof which I had to have repaired at my own expense, not having had enough funds to insure it!

On arrival back in Doncaster I contacted the Crown Agents as instructed by Colonel Bailey, only to be told that the one vacancy which had remained, that which Colonel Bailey had offered to me, had already been filled by them without his knowledge! They had nothing for me. My plaintive letter to Colonel Bailey received no reply and as by this time I had only one month's pay still to come, and hardly any funds left, I decided to apply to the Metropolitan Police who had just introduced their "fast track" scheme. I felt sure I could qualify for this and saw myself with rank in the Met in no time! Down I went for the interview and medical and a ridiculous written examination. All went well although the interview board was somewhat apprehensive having regard to my experience with blacks. They wanted to know how I would respond if I were to be posted to the East End with its large black population. My reply that perhaps I would be better fitted to work with them than others because I knew how they thought seemed to satisfy them and I was offered a post immediately.

I returned to Doncaster to find that the Crown Agents had been frantically trying to contact me because Colonel Bailey had raised hell with them over my case, having given me his word and having sent me back to the UK. They wanted me back in London pronto and within ten days, there I was on a boat, this time the "Stirling Castle" on my way back to Cape Town. I began to feel that perhaps I should buy a season ticket from Union Castle! One benefit of this voyage though was that for some reason I never discovered, I was booked first class and this was indeed luxury.

So, having said farewell finally to Cape Town twice in the previous year, there I was on deck at dawn watching the lights of the city appear once again.

PART THREE – BECHUANALAND 1964–1967
Chapter Thirty-Four

The Bechuanaland Protectorate

Bechuanaland is a very large country bounded on the north by what was Southern Rhodesia, to the west by what was South West Africa, (now Namibia) and to the south and east by South Africa. It is very largely Desert, the Kalahari, and what habitation there is, is mainly situated on the east, along the line of rail. This is where what passes for towns are. The total population at that time was about six hundred thousand, only a couple of thousand of whom were white and six million cattle. The country was known by old timers and residents as "The BP". This being "The Bechuanaland Protectorate". The most northern town was Francistown about seventy five miles from Bulawayo in Southern Rhodesia and in the south, Lobatsi, about twenty miles from the South African Border. Gaberones, now the capital, then comprised only a few Indian shops and a Railway Station. Three miles from the Station was the village of Tlokweng where the Police Depot was. Tlokweng had a few white occupied houses, the Police Depot and a couple of stores and that was it!

The Bechuanaland Protectorate (From Wikipedia)

The Bechuanaland Protectorate was a Protectorate established in 1885, by the United Kingdom in Southern Africa. It became the Republic of Botswana in 1966.

"Bechuanaland" meant the country of the Tswana and for Administrative purposes was divided into two Political entities. The Northern part was Administered as the "Bechuanaland Protectorate" and had an area of 225,000 square miles (580,000 km2). The Southern part was Administered as the "Crown Colony of British Bechuanaland". British Bechuanaland was incorporated into the Cape Colony in 1895 and now forms part of South Africa.

The British Government originally expected to turn over administration of the Protectorate to Rhodesia or South Africa, but Tswana opposition left the Protectorate under British rule until Independence in 1966.

I came off the boat in Cape Town at about eight in the morning and had to make my way to the Railway Station where I caught the train to the north. These long distance trains averaged only about twenty-five miles an hour and

Camels in Bechuanaland

stopped very frequently. Passengers had sleeping compartments to themselves and there was a reasonably adequate Dining Car. The trip to Gaberones took nearly two days and whilst picturesque initially going through the Southern Cape, soon gave way to long stretches of boring flat countryside and semi-desert. The trip was uneventful and arrival time in Gaberones was about two in the morning! I was relieved to see a large white Police Officer, Robin Hardy, going from carriage to carriage until he found me and carted me off the train. He introduced himself and took me to the so-called Gaberones Hotel. It was next to the Station and as there was no electricity, everything was pitch-black and we found our way to a previously reserved room by the light of his torch. He saw my baggage carried in by one of his black Constables and left me, saying somebody would pick me up at eight in the morning. I saw no Hotel Staff at all at this point.

When I awoke in the morning I was horrified to find myself in the most squalid surroundings. I saw that the Hotel was a one-storey building, virtually alongside the Railway track. Steam trains were shunting back and forth, there were hundreds of noisy, very poorly dressed blacks milling around and next to the Hotel was a butchery attended by countless flies. I learned in time that Bechuanaland was home to millions and millions of flies and they were a great problem. Due no doubt to the large numbers of cattle there. I had breakfast in the Hotel dining room and shortly afterwards a Superintendent arrived to take me to the Depot. I was used to Zomba Police HQ, and although in a poor country, was a hive of activity with a wealth of equipment compared to the Depot in Gaberones. I began to realise what a very poor country Bechuanaland was and how terribly equipped the Police Force was. I was attested and fitted out with my uniform and other equipment and given a tour of the Depot together with a general 'run-down' on the country as a whole. I learned that the BP Police numbered little more than one thousand with about forty white expatriate Officers. There were not many fully fledged Police Stations in the country, rather "Police Posts", or sub-Stations belonging to the larger Stations in the main settlements. Very few vehicles could go into the deep desert in those days and around the edges of the desert transport was either by Horse – or by Camel!! The Force owned a Camel Breeding Station with about four hundred Camels on it and Policemen stationed in the really deep areas had to learn to ride them The two main Stations with Camels were Verda and Tsabong and to be posted to either was considered a punishment posting! The Depot had quite a large stable with about sixty horses in it, used for ceremonial occasions and to supply the outstations. I was told I was to be posted to Francistown which had a fairly large Police establishment with an Assistant Commissioner at the Northern Divisional HQ and a full complement of all branches, Uniform, Special Branch and C.I.D. I was to be sent there initially to be orientated into the Force and the country and subsequently would be sent to my own Station somewhere.

At five the same afternoon I was once more embarked by rail for the overnight trip to Francistown. I travelled on what was called "The Mixed Goods" which deserves some time being spent on it. "The Mixed Goods" was exactly what it sounds like, a train comprising mainly goods wagons with two or three passenger coaches and a dining car tacked on. It was an excellent way of travelling from one end of the country to the other with no hassle and was much used by Government Servants visiting either Gaberones or Mafeking. It was run by Rhodesian Railways and went from Bulawayo to Mafeking in the South, stopping at most of the small Railway Stations along the way. In time I travelled on it many times and it was an experience in itself. One had one's own compartment called a "Coupe" with two seat/ bunks in it and a washbasin in the corner. In the evening a Steward came round and made up a super bed, following which, if not already there, one went along to the Dining Car. The Dining Car comprised along one side a Bar and a kitchen and the barman doubled as the chef. Along the other side of the car were tables for four, the usual railways type of table. There were never more than eight or nine passengers, almost always male – and the train staff. A very convivial atmosphere prevailed, becoming more convivial as the evening progressed. At an indeterminate point, i.e. when it was ready, the Chef/Barman would say something like, "Grubs ready", and we would all sit down to a very excellent meal. It always amazed me the meals they could put together. There was no choice – you got what he cooked!

I used to wonder at the considerable numbers of staff there seemed to be and found that because it was a long journey the train carried a double crew. Imagine my concern therefore one night when I was talking to a chap who said he was the driver and he pointed out the other driver sitting a couple of places away tucking into his beers. I asked, "Who the hell is driving the train then?" and he said casually that probably one of the spare firemen was somewhere around! I still slept well!

Chapter Thirty-Five

Francistown B.P.

Francistown
(From Wikipedia)

Francistown is the second largest city in the Country and often described as the "Capital of the North". It is located in Eastern Botswana, about 400 kilometres (250 mi) North-Northeast from the Capital, Gaborone. It is located at the confluence of the Tati and Inchwe rivers, and near the Shashe River (tributary to the Limpopo) and 90 kilometres from the International Border with Zimbabwe.

The Town was founded in 1897, as a settlement near the Monarch mine and named after Daniel Francis, an English Prospector who acquired Prospecting Licences in the region in 1869.

The train arrived in Francistown at about seven in the morning and on first sight it looked quite a pleasant little place. After Lobatsi it was the largest town in the BP in those days and was the Headquarters for the Northern Province. I was met off the train by one of my future colleagues, Cyril, (known as "Squirrel") Ormsby and he took me in his little pick-up to the Grand Hotel in Francistown. What a misnomer! I started to change my impressions of the Town even as we drove from the Railway Station to the Hotel and I could get a closer look at the place. The main Railway Line from Cape Town to the North ran straight through the centre of the town and on the eastern side of the track were a few stores and Government Offices together with the Police Station. Across the line was the residential area, comprising the type of Government housing to be seen anywhere in Central and Southern Africa. There was a Club, of sorts, with a nine-hole golf course and the two Hotels, the Grand where I was accommodated and the Tati, equally squalid. The one road which ran through the town was not tarred and there were quite a number of stray donkeys wandering around, scavenging at the back of the stores and in dustbins. It wasn't even a 'One Horse Town' – just a 'Few Donkeys Town'! Everything was bone dry and there was little vegetation, what there was being covered by dust. I was to learn that it rained very infrequently in the BP and some years didn't even rain at all!

Cyril left me at the Hotel telling me he would pick me up in the morning and take me to the Police Station. It was hot – really hot and there I was at about nine in the morning, a Sunday, in this dirty little town, knowing nobody and with nothing to do. I ventured out to walk round and see what there was to see but there was nothing so I was soon back in my Hotel room. Horrified at what I had come to. Even in later years I didn't change my opinions of the towns. Bechuanaland has a strange, sometimes almost weird, quality about it and there is in this a kind of beauty itself. The desolation in the desert, the evening skies, the rain when it does come are all often breathtaking – but the towns. Ugh!

Early the next day Cyril picked me up as promised and took me to my new work place. There I met the Officer Commanding, a Superintendent named Jock Moncur, (behind his back "My dog" – work it out), three other Uniformed

Inspectors/Chief Inspectors, a CID Inspector, a CID Superintendent and a Special Branch Inspector. They seemed, and were, a very pleasant set of chaps although I thought Moncur had a bit of an attitude. I learned later from the others that he had been very apprehensive about my coming as I had held the same Rank which he now held and he feared that I might be difficult to control. He didn't realise I was just happy to have a job and wouldn't have cared if I was simply a Bugler so long as they paid me! He took me over to Divisional HQ to meet the Assistant Commissioner-in-Charge, Alex McDermott and I was surprised to learn that he was addressed as "Capt. McDermott". It appeared that in the past Ranks in the Bechuanaland Protectorate Police, (B.P.P.), had all been Military and when a change was effected to the more usual Police Ranks, several of the more senior ones opted to retain their Military Ranks. There were I think about five or six and even the Deputy Commissioner was "Capt. Clark". The Commissioner was "Colonel Bailey" but his Rank derived from a previous Military position. What a circus!

Anyway, in a couple of days my uniforms had been altered and I took up my job which was that of Investigations Officer initially. As a matter of interest, the uniforms were identical to those of the Nyasaland Police except that our caps were khaki as in Army Officers' caps and our Sam-Browns and leather work were brown. We had worn black caps in Nyasaland and black leatherwork.

I soon realised what a poverty stricken place Bechuanaland was and this showed in the equipment we had to work with. I don't think I ever saw a paper clip all the time I was there and files were often held together with a spent match thrust through them. Our vehicles were totally unsuitable for the terrain, being one clapped out Land Rover and otherwise one and a half-ton Bedford trucks. Radios were unheard of and so contact, once one was away from the town was impossible. The black inhabitants were in the main, indescribably poor.

Apart from one stretch through Lobatsi there was no tarred road. The main road from north to south was a fairly wide sand road and in parts the sand was so deep that private cars had difficulty traversing it. The main, and most successful modes of transport in the BP were heavy trucks, often of American origin with very wide tracks. They beat out a road which had in the middle what was called a "middle mannetjie", in Afrikaans, a "middle man". The big wide-tracked vehicles ran with a wheel each side of the "middle mannetjie" and one would leave the road to allow another to pass. This worked fine unless you were in a narrow-tracked British vehicle whereupon you drove with one wheel up on the "middle mannetjie" and one in the furrow. Very. very uncomfortable, especially if one had to travel several hundred miles.

Apart from the expatriate Government Servants, the white population were almost exclusively Afrikaans speaking farmers originating, and often from, South Africa, by then commonly referred to as "The Republic". They had little time for "die Engelsmen", (Englishmen), and some of them could hardly even speak English.

I had been there for only two weeks when Moncur told me that I would have to go to a place called Mpanda Matenga, right up in the north of our area on the border with Southern Rhodesia, near the crossing of the Zambezi called Kasane, later well known as a major crossing point for Terrorists en-route to the Republic. I had to go there to meet the District Commissioner, a chap named Phillip Steenkamp, in his role as a Magistrate, to prosecute about twenty Bushmen who had been caught poaching giraffe. This didn't sound bad as Moncur said it would provide me with a chance to get to know the BP better. Then he told me I would have to travel by Land Rover over what was known as the "Hunter's Trail". This was a track which started at Nata, about one hundred miles west of Francistown and wound its way north to the Southern Rhodesian border. This was about one hundred and twenty miles away and there was nothing but hunters' camps between Nata and Mpanda Matenga. I was to be accompanied by a Constable Horapoleng who was also a driver. Off we went one Saturday afternoon, in the Land Rover, with no radio and Moncur said if I hadn't reported back by Police Radio from Mpanda within a week, they would come looking for me! I couldn't understand why, as I left, I had been told to meet Steenkamp only the next Wednesday. But once we left Nata and turned north, I began to see why. The road was very, very narrow and deep sand.

Often we would cover only ten or twelve miles in an hour and we were frequently stuck, having to employ sand-mats to extricate ourselves. Game was aplenty and I shot a couple of buck for the pot and we saw many elephant. The first night arrived and we were miles and miles from anywhere. I didn't know where we were going to sleep when suddenly we saw a very smartly painted wooden sign on the side of the road saying "Kerr Downey". I knew that this was a very large Safari concern based in Nairobi and I had heard they were moving into Bechuanaland, there being so much game remaining there. We turned off the road on an even smaller track and after about a mile came upon this very well appointed camp in the middle of the bush. They even had an electric generator! The camp boys were highly trained, being accustomed to attending wealthy American and German clients and a dozen or so of them turned out and took us over. They unpacked our vehicle, took the buck I had shot and butchered them, led us to hot showers and subsequently beautiful tented accommodation with sheets and mattresses!

They cooked a superb meal for us which we ate at a proper table with white linen and silver utensils. Amazing service, all with many smiles, so deep in the bush. The following morning after a huge breakfast, we left them to await their next, (paying!), clients and continued on our lonely way.

The road, although it ran fairly straight north, in fact made its way in and out of Southern Rhodesia, the border not being in a straight line and as we got further north we began to drive through the back of Wankie Game Reserve in Southern Rhodesia and the game became even more prolific. For the first time in Africa, I saw all of the Big Five, on the road, in one morning. The Big Five being lion, leopard, elephant, buffalo and rhino. This was very exciting for me and of course, half the reason for being in Africa. I have had this happen two or three times since but only in the Kruger Game Park in South Africa. One is very fortunate to do this and often people spend days in one of these areas and see perhaps only one of the Big Five.

The next night we spent at a place called Tamafupi, this being a Government Game Camp, not for hunting purposes but for passing Game Rangers or people such as us to overnight in. What a difference though. No beds, no running water, no toilets or showers. There was however a "pan", (A natural basin or depression in the ground, often containing mud or water), about five hundred yards away with excellent duck shooting.

The next night we arrived at Mpanda Matenga and met the District Commissioner. I was incensed because he had done the trip through Bulawayo on tarred roads in just over a single morning. He said there was no way we were going to camp at Mpanda Matenga so we back-tracked along the tarred road to the Baobab Hotel at Wankie in Southern Rhodesia and once more slept in comfort. When I later asked Moncur why I couldn't have gone the same way he said it was an opportunity to perform a patrol and to show me the BP!

The next morning we went back to "Panda", held the Court, sentenced the poor Bushmen to a short term in jail and off we went on our separate ways, Steenkamp to be back home by the evening and me to spend three more nights under the stars. With my previous experience under my belt I made for the "Kerr Downey" camp the second night and got there to find that a group of American clients had arrived and were in residence. This was apparently no problem however and I was made, if anything, even more welcome. For the Americans it made their Safari even more authentic to have the local Policeman appear out of the night to join them at dinner!

I was intrigued to find that they were often moved from Camp to Camp in the Northern Crown Lands to shoot specific trophies. Say they were contracted with "Kerr Downey" to shoot the Big Five. "Kerr Downey" had scouts out in all their areas and they might shoot an elephant from this Camp today and in the afternoon, the scouts elsewhere would report by radio the presence of a leopard near another Camp. Immediately the clients would transfer by light aircraft to the new location and so on until they had the trophies they wanted. I have to say that this was not my kind of hunting, in fact I never shot anything which was not for the pot or in protection of life or property.

Chapter Thirty-Six

In the Makari-kari with "My Dog"

In spite of having sent me on this trip to let me get to know the BP, Jock Moncur decided that he would impress me with his bushcraft, knowledge of the BP and, most importantly his new vehicle. He had purchased a beautiful new all white Chevrolet one and a half ton truck with fitted fuel tanks for long range trips and a fitted water tank. He carried an additional forty four gallons of petrol and forty four gallons of water in concealed tanks on the back. An almost ideal vehicle for the BP, had it had four wheel drive, and other survival tools, as simple as a spade! However, he was very proud of his truck and said we would go on a patrol to Nata and then across the top end of the Kalahari, what was known as the Makari-kari, (now known as the Mgadigadi), a vast salt pan, to a spot called the Sua Spit where his friend Tim Nangle and his wife, who were working for Roan Selection Trust prospecting for diamonds, lived. They had a large camp there, well established, and the trip was really so he could visit his friends. I had no problems with getting out of the office and seeing more of the BP!

So one bright morning, off we went in the "go anywhere" vehicle accompanied by Constable Matsoberane, the Divisional Cobbler! Why he was selected I do not know. I had my rifle and my shotgun with me and we hoped to shoot something for the pot on the way. I will digress yet again to explain that around the edges of the Makari-kari was one of the great concentrations of plains game in the country and I once saw a herd of wildebeest which the Game Department estimated from the air was twenty five thousand strong! Another time a herd of red hartebeest estimated at fifteen thousand. There was an utter abundance of game by the Makari-kari. The first day we reached Nata, in great comfort in the "go anywhere" vehicle and turned north to spend the night up the Hunters' Trail with which I was already familiar. I had shot a guineafowl and we cooked this in a pot and had a very pleasant supper accompanied by generous tots of "dop" as brandy was called there.

The next morning early we turned back south through Nata. Along the

The Makarikari Salt Pan

banks of the Nata River and eventually onto the Makari-kari. What a spectacle this presented. A vast expanse of white salt extending as far as the eye could see. In the far distance trees were visible which Jock said were on the far side of the pan. How wrong he was. It used to be said that on the Makari-kari at any one time one could see at least seven mini-tornados, in fact very large dust devils stretching right up into the sky and this seemed to be true. We drove onto the pan and found it to be covered with vehicle tracks leading off in all directions, certainly not making a road. We soon found that the trees Jock had thought were on the far side of the pan were in fact mostly mirages and indeed most of what we could see was a mirage. Now and again we would find a solitary post sticking up out of the salt with a reference number on it and these represented sites where RST, (Tim Nangle), had drilled to obtain specimens for analysis. Jock showed great confidence and drove gaily across the salt until suddenly the back end of our truck went through the salt crust into mud. I should explain that although the Makari-kari was a salt flat, if it rained elsewhere it used to flood to a depth of about a foot or eighteen inches and suddenly support a wealth of duck, geese and flamingo. I have never before or since seen so many flamingos at the right time of year, if it rained.

We climbed out of the "go anywhere" and Jock told Matsoberane to get the spade out to dig us out. We then discovered that on this magnificent desert vehicle, there was no spade. Also no sand-mats – an essential to travelling in the desert. We had no option but to jack the truck up, using a cast iron frying pan as a base for the jack, and start digging with our hands. We took it in turn and when we considered we had dug deep enough, climbed out and put a tarpaulin under the rear wheels. The truck just spat the tarp out of the

Flamingos on a shallow African lake

back and we had to start again. This happened time-and-time again and one time as I was climbing out from under the truck, I noticed that the top of the differential was considerably lower than the level of the salt outside. The truck was at an almost forty-five degree angle and I said to Jock that we had no chance of digging it out.

Matsoberane pointed to a stand of trees apparent on the horizon and said he was certain that was Sua Spit where we would find Tim Nangle. He volunteered to walk for help. As we had no radio and Jock had thoughtfully failed to tell anybody where we were going AND we were not on a road but in the middle of the pan, there seemed little choice. We found some bottles in our gear, filled them with water for him and off Matsoberane went towards the tree line. The desert air was so thin and fine that we could still see him walking three hours after he left us which was about two thirty in the afternoon.

The Makari-kari is pure desert, not a scrap of vegetation or life. No insects even and no game tracks of any kind. We could not therefore even light a fire without finding some wood and we remembered that just before we got stuck we had passed one of Tim Nangle's prospecting sites with a Mopani pole surmounted by a sign. We walked back to the site and found about two dozen empty Castle beer bottles – and stole the sign!

As darkness fell we made a fire and cooked a second guineafowl I had shot before we hit the pan. The sign pole gave us just enough wood to cook it. After we had eaten we were sitting around our little table, drinking more "dops", confidently awaiting the arrival of Tim Nangle either that night or early the following morning. We had a little electric light bulb connected to the truck battery giving us light and we were very comfortable. I was sitting facing the direction Matsoberane had disappeared in and Jock was facing me, i.e. in the opposite direction to where Matsoberane had gone. Suddenly Jock shot to his feet and said "My God!!".

His face was ashen and he was looking over my shoulder. Our colleague Matsoberane staggered out of the darkness and said, "Morena, (Bwana) I am dead", and he collapsed. We got some brandy down him and he revived somewhat and told his story. The clump of trees he was making for had never materialised and maintained their distance from him. After about five hours he realised that they too were a mirage and so he turned and retraced his steps. Darkness caught up with him and he stumbled on in what he thought was the right direction. It was, but he would have walked straight on past us had he not looked over his shoulder and seen our little electric light. Had he not done this, he would have continued walking into the middle of the Kalahari and would probably never have been seen again.

We had a "Council of War" and recognised that as nobody had the slightest idea of where in Bechuanaland we were and we had no means of contact, our only choice was to walk. We went back to the prospecting site and carried as many of the empty beer bottles as we could back to our camp. There we filled them with water from the huge tank on the "go anywhere" and to cork them, we used potato, of which we had plenty. We fashioned a kind of back pack from our great coats, which fortunately we had with us and at four the following morning we set off to walk back to Nata, a distance on the truck odometer of forty two miles, leaving Matsoberane to "guard" the vehicle. From what I know not! Finding the direction was easy enough because we simply followed our own spoor. At first the walking was quite easy but as the sun got up it got progressively more uncomfortable. Eventually we found later that we were walking in a temperature of one hundred and eighteen degrees Fahrenheit! We reached the edge of the pan sometime around midday and then walked through savannah type country where lion were far from rare. We finished our water quite early in the morning and thus became progressively more dehydrated. I started to hallucinate and imagined myself walking between two high mesh wire fences. At one point I looked up and found myself about six feet from a buck standing in the middle of the track looking at me. We were so far gone that it perceived no danger from us. Eventually after about about fourteen hours, we suddenly realised we were in the middle of Nata. We made for the nearest Indian store and filled ourselves full of Mineral Water. Then we commandeered the first vehicle we could find and requested the driver to take us to Tim Nangle at Sua Spit. We arrived there at dusk looking and feeling very sorry sights and of course Tim laughed his socks off at us. We must have looked a sight, covered from head to foot in white mud from the pan, very tired and not a little frightened. Tim knew exactly where our vehicle was because we had remembered to bring the number off the sign with us.

We had a glorious shower and put on clean clothes he loaned us following which we sat down to a beautiful meal accompanied by the number of "dops" requisite to restore us. He said that he would send his boys out first thing in the morning, in a Unimog, a German all-terrain vehicle, much used throughout Africa by organisations which could afford them. They would take sandmats and spades and dig the truck out and after breakfast, we would drive there also and bring the truck back.

His boys went off before we were even up and we were sitting enjoying a full English breakfast when to our surprise, our truck drove into the yard with the Divisional Cobbler, Matsoberane at the wheel. We didn't even know he could drive! What an anti-climax! Tim's boys had driven straight to our truck, avoiding all the damp patches which they knew well and when they got there, with their experience they could see the truck would drive out. What had happened was that there had been a full day's sun on the vehicle and the patch we had dug, and it had dried out totally. They didn't need sand-mats or even have to push it. It just drove out and of course, being on their own patch they were able to lead Matsoberane on a safe route back to Sua. We felt such fools and we crept back to Francistown with our tails between our legs. Nonetheless the story got out and many had a good laugh at our expense. It could have been a very different ending of course and Jock had undoubtedly been foolhardy taking a novice like me into the desert, not being properly equipped and not telling anybody where we were going.

One small point in his defence was that it was quite common for Government Servants to disappear into the desert for two or three weeks with a promise to radio in from some remote outpost, if they got there. The standard procedure was if they were not heard of two weeks after they were supposed to call in, a search party would be sent out. Amazingly I never heard of anybody being lost in spite of not having four wheel drive or radio contact. I did many patrols afterwards around the fringes of the desert, all in a one and a half ton Bedford two wheel drive truck, a forty four gallon drum of fuel on the back and a forty four gallon drum of water also. If we got stuck in the sand, we would let down the tyres until they were almost flat, drive out to firm sand again and wait a couple of hours whilst the Constable we had taken with us for just such an emergency, re-inflated the tyres with a foot pump!

Chapter Thirty-Seven

Gods From the Sky

Whilst I am on the subject of the Makari-kari I will recount a quite unique incident which occurred some twenty years before I arrived in the BP.

The Bushman Murders
During the Second World War the R.A.F. maintained a large Training Base for pilots in Bulawayo, at Kumalo Air Field. On October 4, 1943 a Airspeed Oxford, (serial HN 607). left Bulawayo on a training flight which took it out over the Kalahari. Something went wrong with the plane's direction finder or radio and it flew until it ran out of fuel. The pupil pilots, two in number, (Walter Adamson and Gordon Francis Edwards), seeing the wide flat white expanse of the Makari-kari below them, were able to land safely on the salt. At that time they would have been within a hundred miles of Bulawayo as the crow flies. There was nothing else wrong with the plane, it was just empty and they suffered no harm at all. But nobody knew where they were. Within a short time they were approached by a group of real Bushmen, the "San", who had observed the plane's descent from the fringes of the pan where they were camped. The Bushmen of course spoke no English, indeed they only spoke their own "Click" Language which very few white men then understood. They had never seen white men before and were quite convinced that these creatures were Gods who had come from the sky. Many African tribes believe that if they eat a part of another influential being, a rich man, a powerful man, a wise man or a beautiful woman, they will be imbued with that person's envied qualities. This has always been a very common belief. So they lead the two pilots to their rudimentary camp on the edge of the pan, fed them up for three days and then cut them up and ate them!

Meanwhile of course, the R.A.F. had not been idle. After an appropriate period of time they had started their 'Square Searches' during which they search from overhead in series of squares, increasing in size to cover ever wider areas. They had an idea of the area in which the plane could be and of course they were looking for wreckage. To their surprise, after some days, the plane was spotted sitting in the middle of the salt pan apparently, and in fact as it turned out, undamaged. They managed to land small aircraft near it and were very puzzled by the fact that the two pilots could not be found. Pilots were trained to stay by a downed aircraft as this is the most obvious place for rescuers to look and it could not be believed that they had wondered off by themselves, especially as there were no signs of injury or struggle.

The R.A.F. and the Bechuanaland Police were ill equipped to conduct the kind of search now required and the British South Africa Police, (the B.S.A.P.), from Rhodesia were called on for help. They came down with expert trackers who soon picked up the spoor of the Bushmen together with those of the two pilots. There were still no signs of struggle, nor would any be expected as the Bushmen are a very peaceful people. They were tracked to the edge of the pan where the temporary encampment was found, (Bushmen in any event only ever build temporary encampments as they are semi-nomadic), and the trail continued further into the bush. Eventually the group of Bushmen was found and they quite voluntarily told the B.S.A.P., through interpreters, what had happened. They were quite oblivious to the fact that they had committed murder and cannibalism and were sure they had just eaten some fortuitously arrived Gods!

They were arrested, twenty eight of them, and charged with murder. The case was heard in the High Court at Lobatsi in September and October, 1944 and the Judge, Justice E.M. De Beer, found them guilty. However, in sentencing them he took account of the fact that they had no knowledge of the white men's laws, had in fact never seen white men and had simply acted in accordance with their tribal beliefs. He said it would be immoral and unjust to impose any sentence on them other than to discharge them and tell them not to do this again. They were released and taken back to the Kalahari. This must surely be a murder case unique in the annals of British Justice.

Note
[A full record of the Case and Trial, by Robert K. Hitchcock, entitled "Kuacaca: An Early Case Of Ethnoarchaeology In The Northern Kalahari" can be found at-
http://content.ajarchive.org/cdm4/document.php?CISOROOT=/052550590&CISOPTR=924&REC=3
or
http://ehis.ebscohost.com.libezproxy.open.ac.uk/eds/detail?sid=ed9eeb02-5bd2-453d-9a13-617b3923fe14%40sessionmgr113&vid=1&hid=107&bdata=JnNpdGU9ZWRzLWxpdmUmc2NvcGU9c2l0ZQ%3d%3d#db=edsjai&AN=edsjai.10.2307.40980853]

Anyway, Makari-kari was my first experience of the Kalahari and I think we were very fortunate. We could have died and not been found until one of Tim Nangle's crew passed by. Nobody knew where we were and when we were discovered missing, Rescuers would not have had the first idea in which direction to look. We disobeyed a cardinal rule on being lost in the bush which is never ever to leave your vehicle. A vehicle is not difficult to find from the air but one or two people, walking, are very difficult to spot. Since our adventure I have read of several people both in Namibia, Botswana and

Australia whose vehicle broke down and they walked for help – and died. In that heat and without water, you have little chance of lasting long, or being found soon.

My first Christmas in Bechuanaland arrived and I had long lost the strange feeling of the weather being stinking hot and not having turkey Christmas dinners with the trimmings. That kind of heat does not engender a desire for big roast meals. It was more common to have a "Braai", (Barbecue), with some kind of meat, and if possible perhaps crayfish and/or prawns. What I was not accustomed to was the vast amount of booze which arrived in the Police Station for us!

At the risk of appearing sanctimonious let me say here that I believe my Father was utterly, utterly straight as a Policeman. He always refused even the most innocuous hand-outs on the basis that the next day he might have to "book" the giver for something. Even in those days, his attitude in the English Police was unusual. Most Policemen, expected, and received Christmas gifts from various people in the town, especially C.I.D. I'm not talking anything massive, perhaps only a bottle of whiskey or a crate of beer, perhaps a turkey or a goose. None of these ever reached our house and in honesty I doubt my Father received any credit for his attitude. They probably thought he was a bit soft – but he could go for anybody he thought guilty without fear of anything coming out. I am honestly proud to say that I followed his example and never ever took a back-hander in any form.

So when all this booze arrived in Francistown Police Station from local traders and businessmen, just before Christmas, my colleagues started sharing it out and of course included a share for me. I politely refused to have anything to do with it and for sure, they thought I was being unutterably prudish – and took my share. It wasn't long before we were obliged to arrest one of the local traders for receiving stolen property and he had been one of the major donors of the "Christmas Goodies". In fact this didn't stop anybody from proceeding against him, but I personally would have felt very uncomfortable doing so.

Chapter Thirty-Eight

Explosive Wenela

The Gold Mines in the Republic of South Africa got the major percentage of their underground workers from the Northern Territories, namely, Northern and Southern Rhodesia, Nyasaland, Bechuanaland and South West Africa. Manpower was, and still is, a major export from these countries even today. The mines created a Recruiting Agency called the "Witwatersrand Native Labour Association", (known as "Wenela"), and they had large depots throughout the territories in which they recruited. They would embark on continuous recruiting drives and persuade local males to sign a contract for a fixed period of time, usually about three years. After a basic medical examination and documentation, the recruits would be gathered together and flown down to Francistown where "Wenela" had a very large establishment. This was by no means 'Slave Labour' and in many ways was an excellent thing. The system provided employment for vast numbers of people who would never have worked in their own territories, they earned foreign currency and the mine organised an account for them from which they themselves received a disbursement each week, a portion went into savings for them to be refunded at the end of their contract and a monthly remittance went back to the man's family for their upkeep.

At the end of the contract, the man would flown back to his village, a big man, having travelled widely it was believed. He would almost always buy a brand new bicycle with which he returned in triumph and a couple of large brightly checked suitcases with presents for his family and friends. It was a very desirable thing to work on the mines and indeed, when I was at Kasungu, I had a very old hunting boy at Linyangwa, Isaac Banda, who was one of the most courteous and gentlemanly men I have ever met, and in his youth

A "Wenela" Skymaster - somewhere in Africa

he had walked from Linyangwa all the way to "Migodi", (Johannesburg), to work on the mines. There was no "Wenela" then. He had not walked along roads but through the bush and must have walked the best part of fifteen hundred miles!

So, when they reached the "Wenela" depot in Francistown they had a more rigorous medical and were allocated to specific mines and then flown on to Johannesburg by "Wenela" which owned its own fleet of planes operated by a separate company owned by them and called "Africair". They operated DC3s, (Dakotas) and DC4s, (Skymasters) and I will come back to these later.

I have said that the "Wenela" arrangement and contract was good for the Africans and in most ways it was. However there was a big downside, which still exists to this day in that the men were accommodated in hostels on the mines, for men only. No women except those smuggled in for sex. They were away from their families for three years and had no access to women for three years. This of course was iniquitous and gave rise to massive homosexuality. This added to the faction fights between members of historically opposing tribes, still going on, made life in the hostels very unpleasant. In these days of course with the upsurge of AIDS. the mine hostels are one of the biggest sources of AIDS in the world. Some attempt has now been made to provide married accommodation but the logistics and cost of this are exorbitant.

In addition it could not be said that safety was the best on the mines and many accidents occurred over the years, often resulting in the death of hundreds of black Miners.

On my arrival I was appalled at the state of the Charge Office in Francistown and the way it was run. It was without doubt the most disorganised set-up I have ever seen in a Police Station. The Duty Constable would make such entries as he deemed necessary in the Occurrence Book on an occasional basis. The Occurrence Book is a valuable record and should show everything that happens in the Charge Office, who comes in, what they want, action taken and so on. The Lost and Found Property Register was an absolute joke as was the Prisoners' Property Register. One day when I was Duty Inspector I was having a roust round when one of the "Wenela" pilots whom I knew came in. He was carrying a cardboard box and he said, "Here is the latest delivery!". I looked into the box and saw that it contained many sticks and packs of various kinds of explosives, plus rolls of detonator cord and actual fuses. I asked him where this had come from and he told me the story. When the miners from the north were about to be repatriated, before they left the mine accommodation they and their property were searched, supposedly very thoroughly. Pieces of gold ore would be found and often explosive materials. These were confiscated and they were sent back to Francistown for final debriefing and documentation and onwards transmission to their home area.

It appeared that most of them were so frightened on the aeroplane that they sometimes went berserk. They were totally unstable and the door between the cockpit and the passenger accommodation was permanently welded shut to ensure the safety of the two pilots. Seating was very rudimentary, of a canvas military style and the passengers were crammed in. Many of them were sick and/or defecated. One can only imagine the state of the inside of the passenger compartment on arrival in Francistown. A team of cleaners and disinfectors was employed and the plane was first searched. Concealed in various places around the cabin would be all the explosives brought into the Police Station. On every plane! The pilot said they would wait until they got a nice box full and then bring them into the Police Station.

This was not recorded in the Occurrence Book and I asked the Duty Constable what happened to it. He told me casually that they just put them in the big box under the counter. I told him to get the box out and looked inside. I nearly dropped dead from heart failure. It was a big cardboard box about three quarters full of every type of explosive imaginable. And the condition of it was what frightened me most. It smelled awful and a lot of it was very old and sweating. Anybody who knows anything about explosive knows that when it starts to sweat it is becoming very unstable and needs very little to set it off!

I sent the Constable to fetch Jock Moncur immediately and when he came he expressed the same kind of dismay I was feeling. He said he had no idea it was there! I would have thought that being Officer Commanding for over a year he would know what and where everything in his Police Station was. We were faced with the problem of how to dispose of it. There were no explosive experts in Francistown, at least not official ones so we did not dare take it somewhere and set it off. Then Jock had an idea. At the turn of the century Francistown had been the centre of a considerable gold mining operation. Apparently dotted around the outskirts of the town were very many disused mines shafts which were not sealed off and were very deep. They were in sandstone rock. Jock said we should take the material and dump it down one of the shafts. We put it in the Land Rover and Jock and I and another colleague, John Ilsley, set off to find a disused shaft. It was ridiculously easy and we soon saw that the whole area was littered with these big, unfenced holes, with very crumbly edges which went down into enormous depths which we could not plumb. We were very afraid to go too near the edges of the hole because the ground was so soft and crumbly and we could easily have fallen down ourselves. I was amazed that these utter death traps were allowed to be unfenced and not even have any signposts. They were just in open veld and apparently it was quite common for drunken Africans to fall down them and never be seen again. Also what an ideal place to dispose of a body! A few months later I did in fact have to go down one of these shafts to retrieve the body of an African which could be seen about forty feet down caught on a ledge. I went down on the end of a long rope with about twenty beefy Constables hanging on the other end. We managed to retrieve the body which had been there for some time but it was not a pleasant task!

Anyway back to the explosives. Eventually we decided to place it as close to the edge of one of these holes as we dare and with a long pole, push it over the edge and run like hell. We did this and never even heard the explosives reach its destination at the bottom of the shaft - and it didn't explode!! "Wenela" were instructed that in future any explosives found were their responsibility and they flew them back to Johannesburg and handed them back to the mines to dispose of.

If it had gone up in the Police Station I think it would have taken most of Francistown with it! Perhaps not much of a loss apart from life! It was not long after this that explosions became quite common in and around Francistown as the South African National Congress started feeling its strength out. They blew up a Dakota on the airfield and they blew up the Refugee Centre. At about this time Ian Smith and his Government declared UDI in Southern Rhodesia and it was of course declared persona non grata by Harold Wilson the British Prime Minister. The British Government built a massive Radio Transmitter, (C.A.R.S.) on a Kopjie outside Francistown to beam propaganda into Rhodesia in an attempt to cause disaffection for Ian Smith. It failed miserably but they were also very afraid that with all the bombing going on, somebody would have a go at the Radio Transmitter. They sent in a couple of companies of the Welsh Fusiliers to guard the establishment, which was heavily fenced anyway. The Fusiliers were accommodated in their own tented quarters but in their off-duty time had the run of Francistown. An enormous amount of ill will was engendered in the town, first of all because the support of all the whites was solidly for Ian Smith. 'Harold Wilson' and the 'British Government' were very dirty words, and secondly because the Fusilier "Squaddies" consorted extensively with the black prostitutes who flooded into the town, seeing rich pickings. It was a common sight to see a "Squaddie" sprawled out on a settee in the Grand or the Tati Hotel with a black whore either side of him, necking away before disappearing around the back of the Hotel to conduct their business. The Police were helpless to do anything and there was a lot of unhappiness, plus, for some considerable time thereafter, starting in nine months or so, a flush of coloured babies appeared in the town, none of whom would ever know their fathers.

It was not a time to be proudly British!

Before I leave "Wenela" and "Africair" I must recount the sad story of my ex-colleague Butch Nightingale. Butch was an ex-Metropolitan Policeman and he took over from me when I left Mlanje. When Independence approached and the Compensation Scheme came in, he took his lump sum and went off to Mt. Hampden Airfield outside Salisbury where he lived in a caravan and spent all his money, and one year, qualifying as a Commercial Pilot which had always been his dream. Once qualified he got a job as Second Officer working for "Africair" flying the mine recruits around. He was very happy and had got where he wanted to be in life.

One day, an Africair Skymaster, fully loaded with passengers, took off from Francistown bound for the Copperbelt in Northern Rhodesia. It got about sixty feet up in the air, the engines failed and it crashed to the ground instantly in flames. It, and all on it, were totally burned out. Butch was co-pilot on the flight. Subsequent enquiries revealed that the black ground staff had filled the tanks, inadvertently, with diesoline instead of aviation fuel!

No further comment is necessary!

Chapter Thirty-Nine

Elephant Hunting on the Shashi

I was not able to engage in much hunting whilst I was in Francistown other than some very good bird shooting but I did have the opportunity to shoot my first elephant and it was a sad story, never to be repeated. Water, as you will have gathered was in very short supply in Bechuanaland and the villagers had to rely on wells which they usually dug near river beds. They often had to go down thirty or forty feet to find water which they then guarded vigorously. The Shashi can be a very large, wide river, and if it rains somewhere, it is one of Bechuanaland's major rivers. The water then comes down in flood, and continues down river where it disappears. The rivers in Bechuanaland are usually dried up riverbeds but the river can still be flowing, deep under the sand. Where possible the villagers would dig in the riverbed, sometimes very deeply until they found water. They would then surround the well with thick barriers of thorn to protect the water – especially from elephant. It was heartbreaking because the elephant would often travel eighty or a hundred miles in the night to find water and if they found one of these wells, they would break through the thorn and drink the water. Unfortunately, apart from stealing the villagers' water they always, because of their size, destroyed the well by tramping down the walls. The villagers then had no water again and had to start all over. They frequently came into the Boma to ask for help and occasionally, the Game Department, which was fairly strong in Bechuanaland because of the vast numbers of game, would go out and try to frighten the elephant away with Thunderflashes or rifle shots. If this failed, they were obliged, very reluctantly, to shoot an animal, which did keep the others away for a while.

This was one of those occasions and the Ranger involved, a chap named Mike Slogrove, knowing of my interest in hunting, asked me if I would like to accompany him. Equipping ourselves with BSA Majestic .358 Magnums, an excellent elephant gun, off we went to the Shashi. The villagers showed us the well they were having trouble protecting, their only well and we set up our camp on the bank of the river, which was about twenty feet above the river bed. The well was in the middle of the riverbed, about thirty yards away from us. We parked the Land Rover on the bank of the river with its headlights aiming down onto the well. As darkness came we positioned it accurately and settled down in the back to wait. At about 1 a.m. one of Mike's boys whispered, "The elephant are here". At first we couldn't hear a thing and then we heard their gentle quiet movements, carefully breaking down the thorn fencing. We positioned ourselves on the front of the Land Rover and Mike switched the lights on. Immediately we could see that there were three elephants, one down in the well and the other two waiting. As soon as the lights went on there was a wild trumpeting and a mad scramble to get away. We let go with all we had and two elephant fell down whilst the other made off. We carefully approached the two downed elephant and found that one was stone dead. The other struggled up as we approached, trumpeting and spraying blood everywhere. I will not go into further detail except to say that it took two hours to die, in spite of our putting several more shots into it. It was utterly, utterly horrible and I would never want to do that or see it again. It wasn't hunting, nor was it intended to be, it was protection of the villagers' life sustaining water – also the elephants' life sustaining water. A simple question of whose needs were more important, Man or elephant and the elephant lost.

When dawn broke, we looked for the spoor of the third elephant and from the blood and the way it was walking knew that it too was badly hit. We tracked it on foot for about seventeen miles and finally caught up with it stumbling along not knowing where it was or what it was doing. We came up alongside it and mercifully, one shot dropped it dead. It was my first actual elephant hunt, although in Nyasaland I had been out looking for them many times, unsuccessfully and nothing would persuade me to go on another. I have said before that I only ever shot for food, or in protection of life or property and this was one of the latter occasions. Millions of words have been written about the comparative needs of man and wild beasts but in my mind it comes down to man simply being too prolific and encroaching on the space the animals need. Surely they have rights too?

Left to their own devices and allowed a free rein in their natural habitat animals do not exceed an appropriate number. The resources of the habitat determine how many animals can live there and they regulate their own numbers. Man interferes with cultivation and development, takes away the natural space of the animals, they then become a nuisance to man and end up being controlled by culling!

Chapter Forty

Ramaquabane

Came the day I was informed that I was to be transferred to my own Station at Ramaquabane. This was on the border of Southern Rhodesia, about fifty miles north of Francistown and about three miles from the Rhodesian town of Plumtree. It was quite a large area comprising in the main white owned farms and I learned to my dismay that they were exclusively Afrikaans speaking. Many were Bechuanaland born but a number had also come from the Republic of South Africa to farm. The District Commissioner, Phillip Steenkamp, who I have mentioned before, was of Afrikaans descent although he came from Kenya and not long after I went to Francistown, I was having a drink in his house when there was a knock on the back door. Phillip shouted, "Come in" and the door opened a little and an educated voice said, "Can a Kaffir come into this house?". Phillip said, "Come in Seretse and stop buggering about", and in walked Seretse Khama, who at the time was simply the Paramount Chief of the Bamangwato, (the predominant tribe in Bechuanaland), but he was also the leader of the main political party, the "Botswana National Party", and future Prime Minister and President of the new Botswana. I had quite a lot to do with him later in Gaberones and found him a delightful character and gentleman. He was married to Ruth and their story has been written about endlessly elsewhere. However he delighted in referring to himself derisively as a "Kaffir", (the Afrikaans word for a black man), and it used to drive his wife mad!

I moved up to Ramaquabane and found it to be a very pleasant Station, particularly well situated in that I was able to shop across the Border in Rhodesia at Plumtree, which was a relatively big village, with well equipped stores and with an excellent Club which I joined. I was able to play squash and tennis again and still had ample hunting on my doorstep. The farmers, as I met them welcomed the local Policeman shooting on their farms and I was never short of meat.

There was very little serious crime and what there was consisted of mainly assaults amongst farm staff, pilfering by farm staff, poaching the farmers' game but the predominant crime was stock theft – 'Rustling'. Most of the farms were fenced and the farmers kept their fences in good repair. Dotted around the area though were little enclaves of blacks who lived on patches of tribal land where they grazed their cattle. Grazing was at an absolute premium always owing to the pathetic rainfall and the cattle's main diet was Mopane leaves which had fallen from the trees. There was surprising nutrition in this and the cattle were usually in very good condition. In fact Bechuanaland beef was always in great demand overseas.

The Cattle were supposed to be branded but many of the black owned ones weren't, or had had their brands obliterated in an endeavour to confuse ownership. Whenever there was dispute as to ownership of a beast, if it could not be decided, the beast would revert to tribal stock and all ownership of the tribal cattle vested in the Paramount Chief, Seretse Khama. There were around six million cattle in Bechuanaland and a very large number of them belonged to Seretse, who held them in Trust for the tribe. It was said that after the King Ranch in Texas, he was the biggest cattle owner in the world!

The Afrikaans farmers used to husband their grazing carefully and rotate their herds but the blacks just put their cattle where they could. They were constantly cutting the farmers' fences and driving their cattle through to feed. This was called "Illegal Grazing" and was a crime, really theft and much ill feeling was generated because the farmers would impound the cattle, which they were entitled to do. There was a Government maintained Pound into which the cattle went until ownership was established and a fine was paid for the grazing and to recover the cattle, but I spent much of my time sorting out these grazing and rustling problems

Being on a Border Post made me also the Immigration Officer and I had plenty of company as there was constant traffic with BP residents passing through on their way to Bulawayo to do a day's shopping. I used to go through myself about once a month but if I needed something between my trips, there was always somebody who would get it for me and drop it off on their return.

I formed a considerable friendship with the BSAP in Plumtree and was always a welcome visitor to their Police Station. In fact, most of my uniform was supplied to me "under the counter" by the BSAP in Plumtree! Ours was of a not particularly good quality and difficult to obtain. If I wanted new shorts, Terylene instead of khaki drill, shirts, socks and so on, they would always obtain them for me from their stores. In return, I was able to obtain hunting for them which they always enjoyed. The Plumtree crowd as a whole, farmers, shopkeepers, Policemen and the Customs and Immigration chaps were a very agreeable bunch and made my job very pleasant. I got on very well with the farmers, some of whom could hardly speak English and they started to invite me to their houses and Braais, (Barbecues). They invited me to hunt on their land, both to keep in with the Police and because I am immodest enough to say, I was an excellent rifle shot. With a pistol, rubbish, with a shotgun, just adequate, but with a rifle, excellent. The Afrikaaners value a good shot highly and would usually give me the first shot because I didn't miss.

They seemed however to be possessed of a wild, almost uncontrollable frenzy when it came to hunting. As soon as game came into sight, they went wild and I have often seen big heavy Afrikaaners easily clear a five strand barbed wire fence in pursuit of wounded animals. In later years I have seen the same frenzy whilst fishing on the sea in the presence of Afrikaaners. Get amongst a shoal of yellow tail or tunny and they go absolutely wild with excitement!

Chapter Forty-One

Corrie Vos

One of my major friends at Ramaquabane was, and still is, Corrie Vos, who now lives in Ellisras in the North-Western Transvaal, (now the North West Province). Corrie was almost permanently on the Game Dept. blacklist, having been banned from hunting for a period of years following a poaching conviction. As a poorly paid Police Officer I could only afford a minimal hunting licence, with limited game on it. One could however add many, many more head of game as "Supplementaries". This cost money which I didn't have so Corrie used to buy my supplementaries and we used to go out with my rifles and shoot. Nobody was going to catch us anyway as I was the local Policeman. This prohibition didn't extend to game on a farmer's own land but it limited Corrie to his own two or three farms and we wanted to hunt in the Makarikari, or around the edges on what was called the Mumpswe Flats where there was a great abundance of game. We had a fine relationship and many enjoyable weekends together in the bush.

Corrie lived in my area about thirty miles from me, at a place called Tsessebe, on the line of rail and as well as owning a few farms, and the local store, had the most wonderful moneymaking concession. Tsessebe was one of the loading spots on the railway for sending cattle to the Abattoirs in Lobatsi, three or four hundred miles to the south. Corrie had the job, once a week, of loading the cattle and sending them off. Anybody who wanted to send cattle to Lobatsi, had to send them through Corrie. I can't remember exactly how much he got per beast but it was considerable. And it only took a morning a week or so!

Now Corrie was one of six brothers, all farmers around the country, and most of them were for most of the time on the blacklist also. One Sunday morning, very early "Daaintje", (pronounced Dyinkie), and Jannie set off from Corrie's place at Tsessebe to go to Daaintjie's farm at a place called Odiakwe, about three hundred miles from Francistown on the Maun road, through Nata. Bechuanaland used to be plagued by Foot and Mouth disease, spread a great deal by the huge herds of wildebeest migrating across farmlands. In an attempt to curb their movement and reduce the incidence of Foot and Mouth, the Government had years before built what was called a "Veterinary Cordon", a fence stretching hundreds of miles down the country and crossing the traditional seasonal movement of the wildebeest. It was said that often during the migration, they would get to the fence and just build up until the ones at the front died from starvation and thirst. Eventually the pile of dead bodies would build up until it was high enough for the ones behind to run over and clear the fence. This was an ongoing situation.

However, where the cordon crossed main roads a barrier was maintained and a Register of all vehicles passing was kept.

This particular morning, not long after passing through the gate, at a place called Bushman's Pits, Daantjie and Jannie came round a corner to find the road full of lion. They stopped, leaped out of their truck and Jannie, who had a 7mm Remington let go a few shots dropping a number of lion. He handed the rifle to Daantjie saying, "You have a go". They kept firing until the road was full of dead lion and there was no more movement. They counted the lion and there were six of them. They loaded them onto the back of their truck, covered the bodies with a tarpaulin and returned, through the gate, to Corrie's place at Tsessebe. There, the lion were skinned, the carcases thrown down a pit and putting the skins back on the truck, they went to Palapye in the south where another brother had a farm. By about eleven that morning, the skins were pegged out in the sun to dry.

In the meantime, a Game Ranger named Simon Holmes-a-Court, later to die in a yachting accident on his way to Mauritius, came along the road on his way to Maun and saw all the lion lion spoor and blood on the road. He stopped to investigate and found the body of another dead lion in the bush at the side of the road. In all the confusion and excitement, they had not even noticed they had killed this one as well. He put it in his Land Rover and returned to the Veterinary Gate where he checked the Register. As soon as he saw the Vos brothers' names he guessed what had happened. He shot out to Corrie's farm at Tsessebe hoping to find some evidence but of course the bodies were down a pit and the skins by this time were hundreds of miles away. Although he was certain that the Vos brothers had killed the lion, he had no evidence at all and the thing died a death. I only learned about it from Corrie after a safe period of time had elapsed or I would have been in a very difficult position! I do not condone in any way this type of shooting, which I would not even deign to call hunting but I tell the tale to illustrate the kind of life which was lived in those days there.

Let me tell you a little more about Corrie Vos, the Store Keeper, Farmer, Cattle Loader, Poacher and so on. He was without doubt one of the most competent men in his milieu I have ever had the pleasure to meet. I never had the slightest fear in going into the deepest far flung bush with him because I knew he would get us home come what may. We have come home with one tyre stuffed hard with grass because we had used the spare. We came home a couple of times with the fan belt running on pieces of leather. He could fix anything mechanical with the minimum of tools and he could ride anything with legs. Including wild wildebeest! He could tell you the weight of a beast or an antelope to within a pound just looking at it and he was very astute business-wise. He is now a retired millionaire having for many years owned the largest bottle store in the Northern Province, the one which supplied the vast numbers of soldiers the South African Nationalist Party kept there to repel Terrorists.

And in spite of all this, he was quite naive and unworldly. I remember once going on a day's shopping with him to Bulawayo, which represented considerable civilisation at that point. After a couple of hours tramping the streets, he took off his shoes because they were uncomfortable and walked round Bulawayo with them hanging round his neck by their laces!

I just hoped I met nobody I knew.

The prime illustration of his lack of sophistication was shown to me when America put their first men into orbit. It was Apollo 7 in October 1968 and the three crew members were Walter M. Schirra Jr., Donn F. Eisele, and R. Walter Cunningham. Whilst they were orbiting the Earth one night Corrie and I were out night shooting in his Jeep. We stopped for a breather in the middle of a dried up river bed and as we did so, I saw the space capsule very clearly in the night sky. The semi-desert air was crystal clear and we watched it from horizon to horizon. Corrie said, "You know "Chrisjaan", (Christopher), Kobie and I are very worried about those three men. We prayed for them in bed last night." I asked him why and he said, "Do you know that that thing is going at seventeen and a half thousand miles an hour? They will never be able to stop it and get it down!". He genuinely believed this and they had genuinely prayed for the Astronauts' safe return!!

Chapter Forty-Two

Horses and Border Patrols

Another thing I was able to enjoy at Ramaquabane was my love of horses. I gradually acquired three horses which lived in the paddock behind the Police Station and near my house which was on the far side of the paddock. I had a beautiful flame coloured stallion named "Vlam", (Flame in Afrikaans). He was huge and powerful and as gentle and willing as a lamb. He was trained to be shot from and would stand stock still whilst I fired my rifle. If I wounded an animal which didn't drop instantly, Vlam would follow it by himself without guidance from me until I caught up with it and despatched it. He was immensely strong and when I got him from Corrie Vos, who loaned him to me for the duration, I cantered him up the main road from Tsessebe, thirty miles, non-stop! He was quite tireless and very, very amenable. I also had a brown gelding named "Vitvoet", (Afrikaans for "Whitefoot"), who was quite a lazy animal and lastly a blue thoroughbred racehorse mare called "Bluebox". She was a nightmare, and in common with many grey mares, was very twitchy and nervous. She was fully trained to race conditions but not really suitable for hacking. She put me off no end of times, fortunately with little damage other than the loss of skin from my face! I was mentioning how twitchy she was in the Club at Plumtree when one of the Rhodesian Immigration Officers named Jack Stidolph said that he had been a horse breaker whilst in the BSAP. He offered to come over and calm her down a little. I was only too glad to accept his offer and one day he came across the border. We saddled her up and Jack climbed aboard, in the paddock. I should mention that Jack was over six feet tall with long legs he could wrap round a horse. All went well and I was pleased to see that she knew she had somebody on her back who was going to take no nonsense. However she worked her way gradually across the paddock until she passed under a very large tree which grew in the middle of the paddock and had long overhanging branches. Being tall, as he passed under the tree Jack was obliged to curl his back and neck to avoid the branches knocking him off. As he did this of course his weight went forward and as she came out from under the tree she let off an almighty buck and Jack went flying through the air. More missing skin! He got straight back on and stayed on but the point was proved that "Bluebox" did not suffer fools gladly.

I did ride her twice in the Francistown Races and she was an utter joy to ride. No nonsense and it was like sitting on a piece of silk. She was beaten only by "Pinnacle", a thoroughbred stallion also owned by Corrie.

I had a long section of the border with Southern Rhodesia to patrol and soon realised that it would be more fun on my horses than trailing along in a Bedford one and a half ton truck. So I used to take one of my Constables who could ride, usually a Basuto, (they could all ride), and I used to set off down the fence for two or three days. I arranged for the truck to travel by more normal roads and meet us at a specified camping site where we would spend the night. This was a very pleasant way of carrying out my Duty Patrols.

Because we had a joint border I used to liaise with the BSAP in Plumtree so that their patrols along the same fence did not coincide with mine. On one occasion however the Member-in-Charge, Inspector Alan Rich and I decided to carry out a joint patrol down to a geophysical border point known as "Point 222".

We set off one morning in my truck accompanied by my driver and one of Alan's Sergeants who had a smattering of the San language. It is very difficult for non-Bushmen to speak the language because it comprises many click and grunt sounds which their mouths and palates are specially formed to make. Communication however is not impossible and some of the groups have had contact with other Bantu Tribes and have themselves picked up some Shona or Sindebele or whatever.

We drove at a steady pace along the fence in a westerly direction, along a track which ran either side of the fence. We criss-crossed the track regularly, thus driving in both territories and our crossing was made possible by the many breaks in the fence caused by elephants. They have no respect for borders. We called in at the occasional village in both countries and paid our respects to the village Headmen, and of course made our unexpected presence known. We saw the occasional buck or small herds of buck, but no elephant although there was plenty of spoor.

At length we found what looked like a very pleasant place to stop and made camp. It was on a quite small hill on an otherwise flat plain and there was a big clump of trees under which we parked. After a good meal and a few "dops" we went to sleep. We slept on our camp beds alongside the truck, (I never slept under cover all my time camping, much preferring to look up at the stars), and the two Africans slept in the back of the truck. They were usually afraid to sleep on the ground fearing a visit from lion or hyena.

I awoke as I always do, just as dawn was breaking. I think the birds wake me. I lay there in my sleeping bag savouring the early morning and I became aware somehow of a presence. Lifting my head and looking round I saw about twenty Bushmen squatting in a circle around us – in silence. They were armed as usual with their little bows and arrows and knobkerries but these were for hunting and presented no threat to us. The Bushmen are a most peaceful people, if somewhat naive at times – viz. the Makarikari episode!

I whispered to Alan to wake up and when he saw the Bushmen he called his Sergeant down from the back of the truck and told him to ask these people what they wanted. The Sergeant struggled with what little San he had and then said, "They have come to help you cut up the elephant Sah!". It appeared that the only white men they were accustomed to seeing were elephant hunters when they assisted in cutting up the animal in return for meat. We explained that we were not elephant hunters but Policemen and they then asked for salt, a very precious commodity for them. We had only a little with us for our own use but we gave it to them and they then asked for matches to light their cigarettes. Which cigarettes I might add were a work of art themselves, being composed of a little tobacco, "Dagga", (Marijuana which they grew), and rolled in any large leaf or any paper they could find.

Alan was a smoker and gave them matches and asked what they did if they couldn't find a white man with matches. They said they made their own fire and we asked them to show us. This is the only time I have ever seen it done although it is not uncommon amongst African people. It was fascinating. Two of them took a thin wand of hardwood about two feet long and a further piece of soft wood, much thicker, about one foot long. They cut a little transverse channel halfway along the thick piece of wood, picked up a convenient piece of elephant dung and from the centre of the dung, fluffed up some of it and put it at the end of the channel. Then they sat opposite each other and alternatively twisted the point of the thin wand in the groove they had cut. As the hands of one reached the bottom of the wand, the other was waiting at the top to continue the twisting. In no time at all the tip of the wand began to smoulder and they put it quickly into the fluffed up dung which began to smoke. They blew on it and it burst into flame and they lighted their cigarettes. The whole operation lasted maybe one minute. We were most impressed and Alan Rich said, "Well I won't worry about lighting my 'fags' in the bush again. I'll just look for a piece of elephant shit!". Nothing else untoward happened on the trip but we repeated it a number of times as it was very pleasant and useful for establishing our presence in the area. Not many years after this when the Terrorist Insurgents started penetrating into Rhodesia, this area became a "No-Go" area in which it was very dangerous to travel.

One of the other major crimes I had to deal with whilst at Ramaquabane was poaching. The farmers had their game poached by local Africans who cut their fences and also the Rhodesian Africans would come across the Ramaquabane River which for a large part of my District formed the border. Towards the bottom of my area was a very large ranch called Bosoli Ranch, owned by the Tati Company. At the request of the General Manager, Paul Mincher, I once spent several days perched on the top of a Kopjie, watching his Farm Manager hunt illegally. When, with binoculars, I finally saw him shoot an ostrich and take it back to his farm, we descended the Kopjie and caught him red-handed. He was sacked and also fined.

Some time later Paul told me that he was still convinced that poachers were coming across the river from Rhodesia and stealing his game. I took one Constable and two horses and we patrolled the ranch, which was vast, for several days. Eventually one day we heard the sound of dogs hunting and made for the direction from which the sound was coming. When we got close we tied the horses down and continued on foot until we came upon the most horrific sight. Three Rhodesian blacks together with about a dozen nondescript dogs had got a huge sable bull cornered on a small rise. The sable was down on its knees having been stabbed with spears a couple of times and they were stoning it to death. To the end of my days I will never forget the sound of those rocks hitting this poor animal. We rushed in on them and they turned to run whereupon I fired a couple of warning shots from my rifle and the Constable shouted to them to stop or we would shoot them. I doubt if we would have done but they certainly thought so and they stopped. I immediately went to the sable and shot it dead, it was in a terrible state and we then turned our attention to the poachers. We made them skin the sable at once and this was an awful sight because virtually the whole of the inside of its skin was a mass of bruises from the stoning. We made them carry the skin and the animal back to our camp, no mean feat and packed up and returned to the Police Station. I prepared a docket, rang up the District Commissioner, Phillip Steenkamp, a Magistrate by nature of his position and he came straight up to Ramaquabane. We held a properly constituted Court in my office and in the afternoon of the day they were caught, all three men were sentenced for illegal entry into Bechuanaland and poaching. They got five years each and went to prison in Francistown the same day. Justice was manifestly done!

Justice was not manifestly done however in the next case I am going to recount for you.

Chapter Forty-Three

The Witches of Tsamaia

A young African man in his early twenties left Bulawayo to hitch-hike to Francistown to visit his family. One of his lifts dropped him at Tsamaia, a village straddling the road about half-way between Francistown and Ramaquabane, right on the bottom of my area. It was a hot day and he was thirsty so he said to an old woman sitting on the roadside, "Have you got water for me Mother?". She said to him, "Come to my hut my son and I will make you tea". Her house was nearby and he sat on a stool outside whilst she and a couple of her equally aged friends who appeared from nowhere prepared the tea. It was soon made and he drank it and almost immediately felt violently ill. He staggered out onto the road and fortunately a passing truck picked him up at once and took him to Francistown Hospital. He was extremely ill and the medical staff deduced that he had been poisoned, either deliberately or by mistake. Under the circumstances he could not believe the old woman had mistakenly poisoned him and when he was recovered in a couple of days, went into the Police Station in Francistown to report that he had been poisoned by the old woman. As Tsamaia was in my area they sent him to Ramaquabane to report the matter.

I sent a truck down to Tsamaia to pick up the old lady and her two associates for questioning. I do not know how old they were because they were so old that births were not recorded in their time. The principal woman said that in her childhood she had seen Chief Cetewayo of the Matabele. I doubted this but if it was true, it would put her in her nineties. I would doubt this also because very few Africans live to that age.

To cut to the end of the chase, after two or three days of interrogation the following story emerged. The women were members of a coven of witches numbering twelve, all women with a male chief who was a wizard! They had been operating for about fifty years and admitted to killing forty two people over that period. They gave us most of the names and the very approximate year the death had occurred. They had killed the people for a great variety of reasons, to make their crops grow, to bring harm to somebody, to make the cattle fat and one reason the principle old woman gave me was to make her attractive to the young men! The worst factor however was that one only joined the coven by invitation, when one of the incumbents died and the entrance fee was to provide a member of one's own family to be skinned alive! The body parts would then be buried in various fields to make the crops grow.

No need in this part of the world for fertilizer companies!

Well, we opened forty two murder dockets, compiled the statements of the witches and details of the deceased people and I sat down to consider my next step. I imagined the amount of investigation to be done, the numerous exhumations where possible, the charging if possible, the immense amount of time to be spent in the various levels of Courts and decided to take the dockets down to my Officer Commanding, John King, in Francistown. We each foresaw that the ensuing enquiries could reach until our retirements. Cases which could not be seen likely to reach conclusion could be closed by the Officer Commanding as "N.F.A.", "No Further Action". King closed all the files in this way and told me to give the old ladies and the wizard a good talking to and tell them not to do it again. This is what we did. You might think it was no justice at all but once more, it is sometimes very difficult to apply the White Man's Law to Africans. Travel in Africa these days is hazardous, but today's travellers "ain't seen nuttin'"

A further case shortly afterwards was also not brought to conclusion but for different reasons – we could not ascertain the culprits other than to know they came from a specific village. We could not arrest the entire village. In those days the roads between centres were so bad and sandy that there was no bus service and the only mode of "Public Transport" was by very large ten or twelve ton trucks run by Joubert's Transport. They would load up with the goods they were being required to transport and then on top of the goods, very, very high in the air, they would load twelve or eighteen passengers with their belongings. (You have all seen photographs of African trucks laden in this way). One particular truck was going from Francistown to Maun, on the edge of the Okavango Swamps. It was a three day journey and the passengers and drivers would just camp at the side of the road at night. One of the first stops from Francistown was at Nata, about a hundred miles distance. The truck stopped there near the market to allow the passengers to buy food and to relieve themselves in the bush. One woman in her mid-twenties went into the bush to relieve herself and did not return. After a reasonable time, the other passengers went into the bush to search for her but there was no trace. After about four hours the driver, assuming that she had gone about her own affairs, and being now behind schedule, departed for Maun.

When the woman did not arrive at her destination her family started enquiries and uncovered the story as I have explained so far. The matter was reported to the Police as a Missing Person and the next Constable on patrol in the Nata area was instructed to make routine enquiries. Nothing untoward was suspected at this time. The Constable however picked up whispers of witchcraft being involved and my friend and colleague John Ilsley was despatched to Nata to make further enquiries. After six weeks he managed to uncover most of the story. Whilst she was in the bush she was seized by the Chief's Messengers, specifically to be used for witchcraft. They took her away, gagged and bound and she was kept in a hut near the market for about three days until the search died down. In fact the searchers had walked by the hut many times.

After this, most of the village assembled on the village football field one night and a witchcraft ceremony took place. The woman was first silenced by a six-inch long mat making needle being stuck through her throat to obtain her silence, and then she was slowly killed. Her body parts were divided up amongst the entire village and buried in the fields to make the crops grow. John was unable to obtain one single witness to the event, not surprisingly, although he heard the story repeated in detail, substantially the same, many times. The exact spot on the football field where she had been killed was pointed out to him and he took samples of the soil. This was sent to the Forensic Science Dept. at the University of Pretoria in the Republic and they confirmed the presence of human fat in the soil. Today I suppose DNA testing would have proved it to be the woman's but it hadn't been discovered then! This case, as I said, had to be closed because we could get no further. I am certain that this kind of thing still takes place in the more rural areas of Africa. Tribalism and witchcraft are still the strongest motivators.

Chapter Forty-Four

Gaberones and Independence

Came the day I was told that I was to be transferred once more, this time to Gaberones. The Country was moving fast towards Independence and a brand new capital was being built in Gaberones, midway between the old Tlokweng Village and the Railway Station. Interestingly it was designed to represent the traditional Tswana village with the Government Headquarters and Parliament being in the centre and the housing being situated in arcs opening up from the centre. The whole, as in a traditional village, represented the head of an ox with the crescent arms being the horns.

My new job was to open up and develop the new Gaberones City Police Station, to develop a Police System and a Traffic System.

I arrived down in the "City" to find it a relative bustle of activity. Costains were the principle contractors and office blocks, shopping centres, housing and completely new tarmac roads were being built! Civilisation had reached Bechuanaland at last!

Gaborone
(From Wikipedia)

Gaberone (named after Chief Kgosi Gabarone) is the Capital and largest City of Botswana.

It is situated between Kgale and Oodi Hills, on the Notwane River in the Southeastern corner of Botswana, and 15 kilometres (9.3 mi) from the South African border. It is an Administrative District in its own right, but is the Capital of the surrounding South-East District. Locals often refer to the city as "Gabs"

The city has no Tribal Affiliation and is close to fresh water, it was planned to be the new Capital in the mid-1960s when the Bechuanaland Protectorate became an Independent Nation. The City is one of the fastest-growing Cities in the World.

The City is the Government Capital as well as the Economic Capital; it is also home to the Southern African Development Community (SADC) a Supranational Organization, hoping to increase Economic Unity.

It was not the first time I had set up a new Police Station. I had done it in Bvumbwe in Nyasaland, but this was a much bigger project. I had to liaise with various arms of Government, the Roads Department with regard to speed limits, road signs and demarcations. I had to set up a Beat System and teach the Constables how to work a Beat. Then with the enormous amount of building going on, there was a great influx of Africans looking for work, and major pilfering and drinking at the building sites. So all the usual Police work was going on at the same time as all this development. It was a very interesting time.

By this time also, Internal Self-Government had been established and Seretse Khama had been elected Prime Minister. The country was still a British Protectorate and the Head of State was still the Queen, represented by Sir Hugh Norman-Walker, the High Commissioner. I came into fairly frequent contact with these two in my position. Whenever there was a State Event to which Seretse had to go, he now had a Police escort and we had a specially done-up Land Rover station wagon for escort duties, Very fancy with actual working radios and highly chromed fenders and wheels. So fancy, it even had flashing lights and a siren! Great fun to drive around Gaberones. I always used to arrive at State House fifteen minutes before we were due to depart and without fail Ruth Khama would appear at the front door and invite me in for a coffee before leaving. I used to sit and chat and without doubt they were a very pleasant couple, and very much in love. Apart from a great sense of humour he also had a particularly African trait in that he only saw wealth as walking on four hooves. The story was that he never had any money because as soon as he got his hands on any, he would buy more cattle. As I have said, he was the largest individual cattle owner in the world although in theory all the cattle belonged to the Bamangwato.

Hugh Norman-Walker was a typical Colonial Governor although he was very approachable. I had known him very slightly in Nyasaland where he was First Secretary. He expressed a great interest in duck shooting of which there was an excellent supply on some "Pans" about fourteen miles from Gaberones. I was often invited to attend these shoots because I had a superb gun-dog, a Weimaraner bitch called "Capucini", or just "Puci", and who is pictured on the front of this book. She never lost a bird or a buck and was in great demand at hunts. I was invited to go with Norman-Walker and on the first occasion I could hardly keep my face straight. I should mention that duck shooting in Bechuanaland consisted of walking the length of a "Pan" or "Vlei", knee, or sometimes thigh, deep in water, one's feet in mud and shooting the birds put up by one's approach. Hence the normal dress was a khaki shirt and shorts, and a pair of what are now called "Trainers", which had to be tied on to avoid their being sucked off by the mud. When we pitched up at State House at four in the morning, there was H.E., as he was called, waiting on the door step, dressed in a beautiful white shirt with a cravat, a navy blue blazer, Cavalry twill trousers tucked into a little pair of half-Wellington boots! I just couldn't see him wading down a "Vlei" and when he got there he certainly had no intention of doing so. He took one look and said, "I say, I'll take up station on the other end of the "Vlei" and shoot the birds you put up as they come over me!" and that was what he did although he shot nothing as by the time the duck got to the end of the "Vlei" they were flying very high and fast.

As we approached him at the end of the first "Vlei", my dog suddenly went into a point into a small clump of reeds in the middle of the "Vlei". I called her off but she was steadfast and held the point. I walked over to her and told her to come off as no bird had flown and I thought she was false pointing. She looked at me with disgust and dived head-first into the clump, coming out with a quite unharmed duck which had been hiding there. She brought it to me and I broke its neck and hung it on my belt. Norman-Walker saw this and called out to me, "I say old man, that's damned unsporting. The bird didn't even fly!" Shame, but a cheap bird not having a shot fired at it.

After these Shoots we would repair to State House where we enjoyed "G&T's!" The traditional way of ending a shoot apparently!

Although I was now a "City" Policeman, I still had a large country area to Police and this took in quite a large part of the Kalahari. I periodically undertook patrols into the desert and found it quite beautiful. The Kalahari is not the kind of desert most people think of when they hear the word, it is mainly a very low scrub with the very occasional "Kopjie" to break up the otherwise flat landscape. The sunsets and sunrises were often spectacular and we used to sleep, as usual, simply by the side of the truck, with no tent. In the winter it gets extremely cold in the desert and I used to sleep on my camp bed, in a thick sleeping bag with my thick greatcoat on top of that. Often in the morning the whole thing would be covered with a thick white hoar frost. I used to start the day wearing about four sweaters and as the morning wore on, gradually discard them one by one. It was sometimes so cold that my fingers would stick to the barrel of my rifle.

We used the one and a half ton Bedford two wheel drive trucks I have mentioned before and carried a forty-four gallon drum of petrol and one of water. We would frequently get stuck in the sandy tracks along which we travelled and the poor Constable would have to spend a couple of hours re-inflating the tyres after we had deflated them to extricate ourselves. It always seemed strange to me that we did not often see much game on these desert trips. Sometimes a few wildebeest or springbok, the odd hartebeest and of course, there was no water anywhere. Many years in Bechuanaland, it just didn't rain at all. And, amazingly, no radio contact. We would often go the entire trip without seeing a single living soul, or sometimes even any game. Solitude indeed – and very de-stressing! The Police Station knew the route we were going on and we were supposed to be away for a week so if we hadn't arrived back, or somewhere, in two or three weeks, the plan was that they would come looking for us. It never happened to me but I did hear of some Veterinary Inspectors being stranded once or twice. Perhaps my experience in the Makarikari with Jock Moncur was my share of this type of thing! Certainly, coming back from a week in the Kalahari, being dependant solely on one's own skills and endurance, was a great contrast to the relative civilisation of Gaberones.

Chapter Forty-Five

Fishing at Molepolole

About thirty miles from Gaberones at a place called Molepolole there was a very large Mission Station run by a legendary Scotsman called Dr. Merriweather. Also at Molepolole was a satellite Police Station under the command of one of my colleagues, Andy Anderson, a typical red haired Scotsman. Not surprisingly he got on very well with Merriweather.

One day we got a telephone call from Andy asking for assistance. He had a report of three Africans drowning down a well in his area. I should explain that a typical well would be dug near a river bed and would be a fairly square shaft about three feet across going down perhaps thirty or forty feet and then opening up into a spherically shaped chamber in which water would gather. Something like the shape of a spring onion. The water was usually drawn by lowering a bucket on a rope from the top and pulling it up. In the event of there being a need to go down the shaft, a typically African ladder was used. This consisted of a simple wooden shaft with cross bars lashed on at appropriate intervals.

In this case, an African man had to go down the shaft for some reason and when he got down to the bottom and water level, he fell off the ladder and seemingly drowned. A second man went down to try and rescue him and the same thing happened to him! A third went down and he too fell off and disappeared from sight. Nobody else, naturally, was prepared to go down the shaft.

Clearly the well had developed a concentration of carbon monoxide which was poisoning those breathing it. This is a common occurrence with wells.

Andy's problem was that he needed a rope at least forty feet in length, and a grappling iron with which to try and recover the bodies. These were not available in Molepolole. I went round to the Public Works Department to see what they could lend me and their first reaction was, "Keep sending them down until it is full and then concrete the top over!!". I might add that they were exclusively Afrikaaners! Anyway, eventually they found that the only rope they had long enough was a supply of the rope used for hanging convicted prisoners in the Prison. They also found a small three fluked grappling iron which they secured to the end for me.

Thus armed I set off for Molepolole and together with Andy went out to the village. A very, very sad sight met us there. On the banks of the dried up river were about two hundred villagers, sitting silently and consumed with grief. For a small village like that, the loss of three of their men in one morning was a great tragedy.

It is a fortunate, or unfortunate, fact that people whose jobs frequently bring them into contact with tragedy or misfortune, such as Policemen, Firemen, Doctors and Nurses develop a sometimes morbid sense of humour, probably a defence to shield them against becoming too much involved in the sad part of their jobs. What follows is an example of this and I make no apologies for it. We were faced with stark tragedy on the part of these villagers and sympathised deeply with them. However, we had to carry on with our lives afterwards.

I asked for a volunteer to go down the ladder again, this time with a rope round his waist for us to pull him up in the case of emergencies. Nobody would come forward, not surprisingly after three of them had already died but eventually after much haranguing a very old man said he would try. We put the rope round his waist and told him to call if he felt any discomfort. About ten feet down the well he started to gasp and we pulled him up quickly. The well was obviously very full of gas.

Andy and I then sat either edge of the hole and lowered the rope down with the grappling iron on the end. We could see one body floating on the surface of the water and so we had to jiggle the rope about to try and hook him. This was a very difficult task as with the shaft only being three feet wide and the hook being more than thirty feet below us, we had very little room in which to try and develop a swing. We were both fishermen and quickly realised that our activity was very similar to fishing. We started joking about "Got one", "I'm in" and so on. All this in whispers with very straight faces because clearly we did not wish to offend the villagers.

Eventually we got one fluke under the man's shoulder and told the villagers to pull. Slowly, slowly he came up the shaft until eventually he was at ground level. One down and two to go! Unfortunately the other two had drifted under the shoulders of the chamber at the bottom and we really had to work very hard to get a little swing on the grapnel to get it under the shoulders of the well. Repeatedly we would feel one of the flukes take hold and would whisper "We're in", only to have the body slip off. Finally we hooked the next one in a most unfortunate way by getting one of the flukes through the top of his legs so that two flukes were at his back and the third passed through the gap under his groin and gripped the area of his stomach. Of course when we told the villagers to take the strain, he started to come up doubled up, bottom first and became wedged in the shaft. We had to get more men on the rope and inch-by-inch dragged the body up the shaft. It frequently became completely jammed requiring even more effort. As it reached the top of the shaft, with so many men pulling, the body came out like a cork out of a bottle and flew high in the air. From the assembled spectators came the universal African expression of amazement, taken on an indrawn breath, "Hau!", (Pronounced

"How"). It was very tragic but I don't know how Andy and I kept our faces straight.

We spent another three or four hours fishing for the third body but failed. The following morning it had drifted into the middle of the well and was recovered easily.

Whilst I am mentioning the rope used for hanging I will describe the one Judicial hanging I witnessed in Gaberones. Having, over the years, been responsible for investigations sending many men to the gallows, I felt a wish to witness the end result of our work, even if only once. I arranged with the Deputy Governor of the Prison, a chap named Johan Scheepers to let me attend a hanging.

The hangman came from South Africa when needed and I did not see his preparations for the hanging although most people have read about what this involved. At the appointed time I was in the hanging chamber with other officials required to attend. There were two men to be executed for murder and it was not uncommon to perform a double drop. The gallows were equipped for this. It was very quick. The two men were brought in with their hands bound with leather thongs. They were walked to the trapdoor and bound back-to-back. Scheepers read their sentence to them again and asked them if they had anything further they wished to say. Neither of them spoke. They were extremely docile and Scheepers had told me that they rarely needed to be dragged to the gallows or to be tranquillised. They seemed to adopt the African fatality of their doom and accepted what was going to happen to them. The hangman hooded them, placed nooses round their necks, adjusted them and stood back. At a nod from Scheepers he pulled a lever, the trapdoors opened and both men disappeared from sight without a sound. There was no cry or crack of necks broken but they both died instantly. They were left to hang for about five minutes and then let down whereupon a Doctor certified death and they were taken away. I would not wish, or need, to witness this event again but was satisfied to have seen the culmination of some of my work.

Chapter Forty-Six

The Really Old Days

I am almost at the end of my saga but will end on a light note after so many macabre stories. The Bechuanaland Protectorate Police was quite an old Police Force in African terms and there were, as I have mentioned, a few of the very old timers left, most of them with the honorary rank of "Captain" although they were in fact Superintendents or Chief Superintendents or above. There were about six of them left at my time.

My immediate Superior was one such, named Captain Vin Mallen. He was a Superintendent, Officer-in-Charge of the District whilst I was Station Commander - Gaberones. He was very close to retirement having joined the force the year I was born in 1936. He was in the process of clearing out his accumulated junk of the years and one day came across his Official Notebooks/Diaries which Officers were obliged to keep in those days. They made fascinating reading. On joining the Force the new Assistant Inspector was given one month's training at the Depot, (obviously a very highly trained Force!), issued with a camel, (yes!), and sent off on a month's patrol in the desert accompanied by a Constable who also had a Camel and knew where to go. They had to carry all their supplies on a third camel. His notebooks recorded days and days of nothing with the occasional entry saying something like "Travelling along … river bank and saw a Kaffir, (or sometimes Nigger). Spoke to him. Nothing to report".

In those far off days of course the dread words, "Kaffir","Nigger" and similar words were not pejorative but merely descriptive. Mallen never learned that the words changed value and became 'non-PC', a description not even invented then and continued to use them.

In the winter when it became very cold in Bechuanaland, he used to get very irate with the Constables and shout at them to get a move on. He would then mutter quite loudly, "God, there's nothing like a frozen Nigger!" Nobody used to mind, they would just laugh at old Captain Mallen carrying on again. The finest example of his out-dated attitude though came when one day he rang me and asked me to come to his office. I have mentioned that as well as being Immigration Officers and Customs etc. we also used to issue Passports. The time I am speaking of was after Internal Self-Government had been granted and we now had a black Minister of Home Affairs. When I got to Mallen's office I saw seated in front of him an African I recognised as Quett Masire, who followed later as President after Seretse died. When I entered, Mallen said to me, "Mr Bean, this Nigger wants a Passport!".

I couldn't believe it. This man was our Big Boss!! I said, "Capt. Mallen, this is Quett Masire, the Minister for Home Affairs". He replied, "Never mind that. Give him a passport".

I asked Masire to follow me to my office and I could see he was laughing. I didn't mention what had taken place and he obviously dismissed it as one of the "old man's" idiosyncrasies. They all knew him. Thank goodness Quett Masire was not sensitive as so many of these people, rightly or wrongly are.

Eventually September 1966 arrived and Independence was granted to Botswana as it then became. There was much celebrating and great festivities. The Queen's Representative for the occasion was Princess Marina and I had much escorting of her to attend to. I stood in the garden of State House six feet away when she Invested Seretse Khama as a Knight. There was quite a sense of occasion.

The Celebrations terminated with a huge ceremony in Independence Stadium with great marching of bands and many speeches. Eventually at midnight we had the ceremony of the lowering of the Union Flag, a very poignant moment, and the raising of the new Flag of Botswana. Flags being hoisted are furled in a special way so that when they are at the head of the mast, a tug on the rope unfurls the flag and of course, everybody is supposed to cheer. In this case, I'm afraid much to the delight of most of the white people present, the flag wouldn't unfurl and repeated tugging failed to release it. It had to be brought down, unfurled and re-hoisted. Many thought it an ill omen but Botswana has prospered greatly since then with the finding of diamonds at Orapa together with other minerals.

I left Botswana very shortly after this, fleeing the black tide. I left Nyasaland when it became Malawi, Bechuanaland when it became Botswana and Rhodesia when it became Zimbabwe. People in South Africa who learned of this, jokingly pleaded with me not to leave South Africa also. I used to joke back then that the only places further south I could go were Marion Island, Gough Island or the Antarctic!!

I never long for my days in the Colonial Police because those times are long gone. I consider myself a most fortunate man to have lived in so many exotic places and to have had such a varied and interesting life. Had I stayed in the UK Police, I might have attained a higher Rank and be a retired Superintendent or even more now, and I might not. But I would never have had the joy and excitement and been able to enjoy such beauty as I did.

After forty seven years in Africa I am settled happily back in England, only owing to the extreme violence one is constantly in danger of in South Africa today. I feel I am relaxed and fulfilled and have come full circle. I am home!

GLOSSARY

"A's and D's"   – Absentees and Deserters Enquiries.
A.D.C.   – Assistant District Commissioner
Administrador– Government head of a district in Portuguese East Africa.
A.N.C.   – African National Congress
Bwana   – East and Central African, originally "Lord", now "Sir"
Boma   – East and Central African term for a fenced-in area, fenced with thorn and now the generic term for the Local Government Administrative area and offices.
Boy   – A non-pejorative word used to describe a person's job, as in "Cook boy", "Garden boy", "House Boy", "Petrol boy" etc.
B.N.P.   – Botswana National Congress
B.P.   – Bechuanaland Protectorate
B.P.P.   – Bechuanaland Protectorate Police
Braai   – Afrikaans for a Barbecue
B.S.A.P.   – The British South Africa Police – Southern Rhodesia
C.A.A.   – Central African Airways
Chambo   – Most common fish in Central and East African waters. A great delicacy. Actually a type of Bream, (Tilapia melanopleura).
D.H.Q.   – District Headquarters
D.C.   – District Commissioner
F.M.B.   - Farmers' Marketing Board
G.C.E.   – General Certificate of Education
H.Q.   – Headquarters
H.E.   – His Excellency, referring to the Governor of the Territory
Kachasu   – Very potent distilled African brew – illegal.
M.C.P.   – Malawi Congress Party
Mfisi   – Hyena
M.O.   – Medical Officer – also Modus Operandi
Morena   – Tswana equivalent of "Bwana"
N.A.A.F.I.   – Navy, Army and Airforce Institute
Njinga   – Chinyanja for bicycle
N.R.P.   – Northern Rhodesian Police
P.E.A.   – Portuguese East Africa, (now Mozambique)
P.M.   – Post Mortem examination (or Prime Minister)
P.C.   – Provincial Commissioner, (now also "Politically Correct"!)
P.M.F.   – Police Mobile Force – specially trained Riot Police.
P.W.D.   – Public Works Dept. Responsible for upkeep of buildings roads and motor vehicles etc.
R.C.M.P.   – Royal Corps of Military Police – as distinct from
R.P.   – Regimental Police
Riding (The)   – The West Riding Constabulary
R.M.   – Resident Magistrate
WENELA   – the Witwatersrand Native Labour Association

THE NYASALAND POLICE ASSOCIATION (NYPOL)

(The Association of the ex-Members of the Nyasaland/Malawi Police Force)

The Nyasaland Police Association was the dream of Christopher Bean and he established it in 2005 from his home in Doncaster in England.

All ex-Members of the Nyasaland Police Force are welcome to become Members as are children of Officers who served and any others closely associated with the Force, i.e. secretaries, Magistrates et al. We maintain a Website at www.nypol.com and produce a Newsletter at regular intervals.

In 2010 Christopher went to the unveiling of the B.S.A.P Memorial at the National Memorial Arboretum at Alrewas in Staffordshire and saw Memorials to other Colonial Police Forces. He felt that the Nyasaland Police should also be remembered in this way.

He organized an appeal and the funds were raised for this. On 21st July 2011 the Memorial was unveiled by Professor Colin Baker and dedicated by the Rev. Canon Don Ruddle, an ex-Member of the Force at a gathering which was attended by some ninety Members and supporters.

NyPol Assn Contact information
Postal Address:
1 Riding Close,
Bessacarr, Doncaster, S.Yorks. DN4 6UZ
ENGLAND.

Tel No: +44 130 253 2589
eMail: christopherandliz@tiscali.co.uk
WebSite: http://www.nypol.com

The NyPol Memorial at Alrewas

THE FEDERAL SAINTS GROUP

(The Pupils and Staff of St Andrew's Schools, Blantyre, Nyasaland (Malawi)

The "Federal Saints Group" was a similar dream, (as Christopher's), held by Ian "Witty" Whitfield. For many years he wondered what had happened to all the School Pupils he had been with at St Andrew's School in Blantyre, Nyasaland (now Malawi), during, mainly, the Federal Period of 1953-1964 and beyond.

In 2005, after retiring, he started in a small way - with the use of the Internet - to look for, and record, all the old "Federal Saints" he could find. In this same year he started a (free) monthly electronic Newsletter which later became "The Federal Saints Journal".

Membership (free) is open to all ex-St Andrew's Pupils and Staff as well as other parties who have an interest or connection with the School or the Country. We now have a Database of almost 3000 names and our "active" members are spread across over 50 Countries round the World.

Our Journal covers all aspects of the History and News of both the School and the Country as well as letters and other submissions from the Members and other related topics and current affairs and News.

We hold Annual Reunions in various Countries round the World and frequent Social "Get-Togethers" from time-to-time at different locations. As well as our Journal we maintain an active WebSite and a presence on Facebook.

Contact Information

Ian 'Witty' Whitfield

Editor of - "The Federal Saints Jounal"
(And Admin of "The Federal Saints Group")
Pretoria, South Africa.
Alternative eMail - federalsaints@gmail.com
Federal Saints WebSite - www.federalsaints.net

The Federal Saints Group

Tel - +27 (0)12-817-2001
Cell - +27 (0)82-573-9142
FAX - +27 (0)86-651-4844
Skype - 'ianzs6cdx' (Get Skype and call me for free!!)
SnailMail - PO Box 72226, Lynnwood Ridge, 0040, South Africa.
Facebook - 'Ian 'Witty' Whitfield

"Doctrina Habet Onus"